Five or Six Characters in Search of Toronto and Other Plays

South Asian Canadian Literature Series

General Editor: Uma Parameswaran

SACLIT 1	**Trishanku and Other Writings** Uma Parameswaran
SACLIT 2	**Sons Must Die and Other Plays** Uma Parameswaran
SACLIT 3	**Five or Six Characters in Search of Toronto and Other Plays** Rana Bose
SACLIT 4	**Land Where the Trees Talk and Other Plays** Rahul Varma

Five or Six Characters in Search of Toronto and Other Plays

RANA BOSE

Selected and with an Introduction
by
Uma Parameswaran

PRESTIGE

Published by
Prestige Books
3/28, East Patel Nagar
New Delhi 110 008

1998

ISBN: 81-7551-021-8

Photo Typesetting by
Pivot Computers
Delhi 110 006
Ph. 2934490

Printed at
Chaman Offset Printers
New Delhi 110 002

Contents

Introduction
An Interview with Rana Bose

Rana Bose is a playwright who lives in Montreal and is the co-founder and artistic director of Montreal Serai, a collective that publishes a magazine and produces at least one major play each year. He was born in Calcutta in 1950, educated at St. Xavier's School, and took his engineering degree from Washington University in the United States. He came to Montreal in 1977, and is now a senior executive in an engineering company. He has written and produced nine plays since 1986. The list includes: *Baba Jacques Dass and Turmoil at Cote-des-Neiges Cemetery* (1986), *On the Double* (1986), *Some Dogs* (1987), *Whom to Please?* (1989), *Nobody Gets Laid* (1990), *The Death of Abbie Hoffman* (1991), *Five or Six Characters in Search of Toronto* (1993) and *The Sulpician Escarpment* (1994).

Rana is an intellectual dissenter. All his plays highlight the theme of protest, not specific injustices or individual incidents of suffering so much as the systemic shortcomings that give rise to and perpetuate an unjust society. In *Baba Jacques*, for instance, he speaks of the systemic ghettoization of the Indo-Canadian community that is both self-imposed, and government-imposed by the policy of multiculturalism. *Five or Six Characters* is a fast paced lampooning of what he calls "tribalism," and he has the action taking place on the highway between Montreal and Toronto, with half a dozen characters representing various tribes. While the Canadian audience would readily identify the tribe of hockey jocks and the political satire, the Indian reader would also see immediate relevance in the fundamentalist who is carrying a brick to build a church in Toronto and in the flatulent literary-criticism jargon of the academic, both of whom are among the passengers in the bus that crashes into the tunnel of Time Zero.

As though the dialogues are not abstruse enough, Rana uses stage effects that are kaleidoscopic. Small wonder that his plays do not fly in a country where racial minorities are not expected to be sophisticated or intellectual when writing about their life in Canada.

The following interview was conducted in his house in Montreal on March 24, 1996.

Uma: I have written about your plays and about *Montreal Serai* in various journals[1] such as the *Toronto South Asian Review* and in *Contemporary Issues in Canadian Drama.* Also, the literary qualities and the political thrusts of your plays can be drawn from your texts if one is willing to put in some critical effort and do one's homework about the political realities around us in Canada. So today I would like to get some background information that only you can give. Tell us something about the early influences in your life that have shaped your literary imagination and dramaturgy.

Rana: When you phoned me two days ago about the questions you had in mind for today's meeting, it set me thinking for the first time about some aspects of my work that I had never consciously given thought to before.

My interest in theatre—I think it started with my father taking me in the late 50s and early 60s to see Utpal Dutt's *Little Theatre Group* in Calcutta at the Star Theatre, and what really overwhelmed me about Utpal Dutt's group was the power of their acting and their visual attack on the senses. Even as a child I was overwhelmed by the power of their theatre. Later I came to know about Utpal Dutt's political beliefs and I couldn't care less. Over the years I have come to have a cynical disregard for unsubtle attempts at using the stage as a pulpit. What came through to me was that Utpal Dutt, like Rod Steiger, or Marlon Brando in *Streetcar named Desire* . . . had a kind of personality, handsome, with a broad forehead . . . an extremely powerful presence.

At the same time, there was something else. Utpal Dutt had a stage craftsman, Tapas Sen; Tapas Sen was an incredible character; even in those days, when facilities were rather primitive compared to what can be done now, he created this magnificent spectacle on stage. I went to see his *Kallol*, about the Naval Mutiny, and he had erected the whole bow of a ship on the stage, and was firing cannon balls straight into the audience; the deck of the ship was on the main aisle, and you could see trapdoors popping open and ratings were jumping out and the rebel navy men rushing forward. It was so powerful . . . and then there was *Neecher Mahal*, the Bengali version of Lower Decks . . . and *Nildorpon*, the Indigo Revolt, another classic. I still remember the great line from that play. When the English forced our people to cultivate blue dye for export, instead of cultivating rice and wheat, the peasants rose in revolt and the war cry was, "This hand won't sow blue dye anymore!" I was five years old then, but I can hear it even now.

The power of the theatre got under my skin as politics; all these were political plays using theatre but it was the theatre part that got me going about politics, the other way around you know, even though there was a long tradition in my family of left wing association. At the same time, there was this cultural thing, I don't mean poetry, dance etc., but a personal culture, meaning an affiliation with one's behavior, values, an open association with a way of life that is multi-dimensional, a blend, a mix of many temperaments—"foreign" and "domestic."

I grew up in a neighbourhood called Elliot Road in Calcutta. By conditioning, I didn't grow up as an urban Bengali boy; I grew up in an Anglo-Indian milieu.

Uma: Why was this? You said in an earlier conversation that your family were left-wing; did that have something to do with where you lived?

Rana: My parents were working professionals. They had travelled abroad, and studied abroad; and my father was working in downtown central Calcutta and we always lived in that part, before my birth in Creek Row and Dharamtola Street, and then Elliot road, and these were all non-Bengali, non-Hindu areas—they were Anglo-Indian, Christian and Muslim neighbourhoods; around the Park Street area, not in the posh areas like Carvac Street and Hungerford Street where many mill managers lived.

My father was a doctor, a heart specialist; besides being a top-notch cardiologist, he was very much a social activist; for instance, the Students' Health Home in Calcutta was founded by him; in our house. The People's Relief Committee, which gave help in times of floods and other disasters, was founded by him. He was the founder of one of several in a group, and now those places are huge—Students' Health Home now has a six storey hospital—but all of them started in a house, our house; my father was into front line grassroots activism, which of course didn't go well with his professional milieu. But he was also President of the Indian Science Congress at the Madras session . . . which was the first time I visited Madras.

My mother was a professional statistician, she was not into politics, she kept out of it because she was a government bureaucrat; but I have a sneaking suspicion that she always voted left, and never told anyone about it. Anyway, I went to St Xavier's School, which was a very anglicized environment; so my cultural upbringing was cross bred, and I didn't go for Rabindra Sangeet and all that; I am not defensive when I say this; I don't think I missed a lot. But at the same time, my father was a doctor for Tagore, and so we were connected to the Tagore family. Despite that, my cultural needs were already embedded somewhat differently. I had a hungry need for doing all kinds of things, and was not interested in being tied to any one kind of culture. I had to have it all, under the belt.

Theatre caught my interest, especially Tapas Sen's lighting . . . when I do my theatre here in Montreal today, I realized, in the last couple of days since you asked me to think of early influences, that the origins of my techno theatre, my nineties theatre, using a lot of techniques, a lot of effects, is actually rooted in Tapas Sen's enormous stagecraft. Those were the fifties, primitive; can you imagine, there was nothing, no motorized strobes, couldn't patch panels together, no computerization, not like now when we have so many dimmers—in an average auditorium today we have fifteen, twenty dimmers, and of course now you have them, all the fancy stuff, in Calcutta too, and yet that man achieved such dramatic effects with next to nothing. Now in the nineties, you see Carbon 14 and Lalala and Human Steps and Edward Locke and their avant garde performance. I am not saying one or the other influenced me. But I am saying that all that came together in my poor man's theatre; it will always be a poor man's theatre because I am convinced that I will never get funding. We don't have the ability; when I say that I don't mean theatrical ability but the political savvy to get funded; I don't know how to lick the right butts; it takes that; I am not demeaning it, but anyway, going back to my roots, there were these experiences of going with my father, and these epic performances, *Kallol* and *Manusher Adhikarey*, which is much later . . . and Tapas Sen's tremendous stagecraft made me politicized much more than the actual politics did; mind you, my family had a lot of left-wing associations, with people coming and going through our house; when the communist party was banned, people came to our house for shelter, and so I'd meet all kinds of personalities, I could rattle off names, but that's not what politicized me; what politicized me was the power of performance. So there I was, not actually into theatre but subliminally affected by the visual attack that theatre gave to the senses; just imagine, you see a flaming jeep on stage and you see a policeman roughing up somebody . . . it makes a permanent mark on you. We didn't have television then. There was no Rodney King being roughed up by police on TV.

So I was still not in theatre as such, though I had this subliminal persuasion. Then we come to the late 60s and 70s, and I get politically involved in the student movement and a lot of things happen on campus . . .

And then, the next phase in theatre involvement took a different turn. While one wanted to be naturally a leftist, and be affiliated with progressive and democratic causes, there was a big cultural vacuum in the movement in terms of political culture; not in terms of activities because there was a lot of singing and dancing and composing and theatre going on but within the organization, there was a culture of feudalism. It was extremely feudal, it was dadagiri. Stalinism is feudal. No matter how industrialized a society is, feudalism thrives. For me feudalism is a power you wield on people; it is an extra-political power, an undemocratic kind of exertion on everybody. Theatre is an outlet; it is liberatory, it lets you do what the dadas and gurus won't let you do; once you are into theatre, you go wild. Then there is that romantic imagery, all over the world revolt is happening, free speech movement, Sorbonne, Berkeley, Berlin, Prague. I knew about Mario Savio in Berkeley when I was in India; and I read the poetry of the beat generation—Ginsberg, Kerouac, Burroughs . . . these expressions may sound clichetic but it appealed to me that words, rhythms, call them bohemian if you will on-the-road literature, appealed to me, in terms of visual and oral attack—jazz poetry that I use today in readings of my poetry in Montreal bistros and pubs, it has roots all in a kind of social curiosity, in my upbringing, my father taking me to see theatre . . . he would never preach, just say "look at this, read this, what do you think of this" . . . all this gelled together, when in the 60s and 70s I got involved . . . I realized that all organizations, even the most radical ones, could be radical but were internally, culturally living within the realm of society, which was semi-feudal; there was no escape from it.

Some of the things that happened in the Naxalite movement had to do with the feudal culture within the organization; very rigid codified guilt-tripping, class-consciousness in reverse. This is a lower middle class thing. . . . An enormous glorification of physical suffering; in the olden days it was said that if you didn't have tuberculosis you were not a good communist, and if you were not dying of hunger you couldn't be a good party activist, but I thought it was more important to do something regardless of background and daily meals. There was all this romanticist energy at work. Che Guevera was not dead, even though in the Maoist movement he was considered totally incorrect. . . . On the one hand there was the genuine affiliation with the working poor, but at the same time there was a need to do things that were powerful; all that romantic energy . . . the storming of the Bastille was like political theatre, like taking the cobblestones apart, bombarding the headquarters, raising flags!

Then when I started doing theatre in college, well I was only marginally involved, mainly because all the theatre was in Bengali and my knowledge of Bengali was not enough; in fact I learnt Bengali only after I left home and went underground; so I hung around like a groupie, helping with stage . .

like when on the street, we needed a lot of workers, literally physically cordoning off the street stage from violent interruptions by holding hands around it, and at this time theatre became an increasingly dangerous occupation. So here was Dutt and Badal Sircar and Rudra Prasad and all the old radicals, and the Star Theatre, and then there was the open theatre, Muktangan, that was increasingly coming under attack under Mrs. Gandhi's rule; the police would come and open fire. In fact one of the most painful incidents in my life was the killing of a good friend of mine when he was acting, while he was on stage, not a stage so much as the street of course, but it was like Hyde Park in those days, and he was shot to death in cold blood by a plain-clothes policeman.

It was at this time that it struck me, that my father, who was the founder of APDR (The Association for the Protection of Democratic Rights) was opening my eyes to the basic cultural need for democracy. It was the beginnings of the civil liberties movement; even we, who were in the left, had no idea of civil liberties, we thought of it as a wimpy thing, to talk of civil liberties, while the armed struggle was going on in Viet Nam etc. but later on I realized that these were the people who were the real bourgeois democrats of our country, my father and his generation, who studied in England in the 20s and 30s, who were trying to introduce the concept of personal liberties and individual rights, that the concepts had to be ingrained. Only Bengali theatre taught me about civil liberties.

Even up to this point, I had been only marginally involved in theatre. I had not done theatre. I had been going outside Calcutta to faraway places, like Khurda, which had a phenomenal theatre movement. It was street theatre and guerilla theatre, and then came the repression. I ended up in jail for quite a long time; I got busted for my student activism. Indira Gandhi had jailed over 30,000 in one shot.

Uma: Was this for theatre activities?

Rana: No, it was for my student involvement. I had acquired

notoriety as a student leader; they amassed a lot of charges against me; at one time, they had something like thirty charges against me. That was typical of the times. The ambassador to the United States now, Siddartha Ray, was the chief minister.

They withdrew all the charges and then detained me on the Preventive Detention Act. Those were very gruesome, very politically educating times, and then I literally had to exile myself. I had dropped out of school for five years and was in a rural area . . . and after I got out of jail, there was no place for me; no college would readmit me. The whole movement had dissipated; I always suffered from ideals of cultural liberation, I think I really believed we could do something; you know what Emma Goldman has said: "If I can't dance I don't want to be part of your revolution"; even though I didn't know the statement then, I knew it was the way I felt. But the liberation didn't happen. I left India at the time virtually as an exile, and I reluctantly started working very hard at an engineering degree and completed it in record time—two and a half years.

At that time, when I was on campus, the Viet Nam war was coming to an end and Watergate was happening, and of course I got involved. That's when I came to know about the technology of theatre and started writing poetry, it was probably quite effete. My black roommate got me into jazz poetry and theatre and then I saw the San Francisco Mime Troupe, and the Vermont Bread and Butter Theatre, and all this revived in me the sense of liberatory theatre but it was not the Brechtian theatre, The Good Woman of Szechwan and all that kind which had impressed me in Calcutta, but this was mask drama and poster drama—all that was going on in the U.S. at the time. I took theatre courses—at Washington University in St. Louis—and I learnt the basics of stage production; I did some stage lighting and designing for a band—Gerry Mulligan's—he was a saxophonist—as part of a course. It made me understand what Tapas Sen was doing fifteen years earlier with the crudest possible devices. Then came the Emergency and I came to Montreal and started writing plays. It was very difficult at first, didactic, poster drama straight out of the seventies. But now it is different. There is this enormous influence of Brecht, to entertain and educate through song and dance, the concept of epic theatre . . . and then there is the influence of jazz and my tremendous affinity for music, movement and imagery. I am also thus propelled towards multi-media theatre and this is where Carbon 14 and others come in.

And now what has happened is that living in Canada and Quebec and Montreal, my world has gelled to a Montrealais environment. And all those years of India, politics, Utpal Dutt, Sircar, my father, the great melancholy I feel for my father's absence in my life even now, though he's been gone for twenty one years . . . my stay in the U.S. all is distilled into Montreal, here in 1996, referendum, tribal politics worldwide. At the same time, I am an engineer, senior executive in a very large Canadian company, and that has brought in a technological bent, a desire for precision, a multi-dimensional cultural edge—to perform on the borderlines and expand the borders. Everything that is happening around us has made me wary of borders. Borders will always exist, but I believe in extending borders, extending and bringing them to the centre, of blending.

Uma: You seem to have your own definition of "blending" that is not used in the usual sense of mixing.

Rana: Blending is for me a kind of political assertion that is inclusive. I feel that I can just as well define the terms of inclusion rather than demand to be included. We have to go beyond making demands to be included. We have to be taking the lead; saying, "Want to join? come on." We should lay the ground rules for inclusion. That way we won't have to worry about being excluded.

Everything we do is political; you can be blatant about it, you can be polite about it, but everything is political.

In the final analysis, I am tired of pounding the audience, but I still do it, I guess it is in my bloodlines!

Uma: In each play you are motivated by that bane of all idealists, the desire to change the world, and you adopt metaphor and satire as your main tools.

Let us briefly talk about two or three specific plays. I would like to start with your first major play, the one with the colourful title—*Baba Jacques Dass and Turmoil at Cote-des-Neiges Cemetery* (1986.) I love the Montreal setting you use. I like the Canadianness of your setting and themes. Universals are okay, but it is the specifics that give life to a piece of contemporary writing. You can see I am trying to shape this interview after my ideology, which is that we should be writing about the here and now.

Rana: It is okay by me because you are one of a few, outside our Serai circle who understands what I am trying to do.

Uma: *Baba Jacques* is your first play and so you have cast your critical eye on the Indo-Canadian community. But there are other targets as well.

Rana: Yes, the first target was the rule about "no dirty laundry washing in the public." The second was about how and why new immigrants were succumbing to the patently patronizing ethno-submersion programme of Canadian multiculturalism.

Uma: That is a difficult balancing act. To deride a minority community on one hand, and to speak about the majority's oppression of minorities on the other. I find that problematic in *Baba Jacques*. Your hero, Binoy, goes on and on about the Indo-Canadian crowd. But you carry it off in *Nobody Gets Laid* (1990). It is about majority-oppression but it succeeds because you are not laughing at minority idiosyncrasies.

Rana: Why would you say that? I am using stereotyping in having four immigrants (Iranian, Greek, Spanish, Indian) boiling with rage in their own cultural dialect against the backdrop of a racist Canadian summer.

But you may be right. The Oka crisis and Quebecois nationalist mean-mindedness come out so strongly that one ignores the stereotyping.

Uma: Spell them out. How did the two political aspects affect minorities?

Rana: First of all there is the Oka incident. White racism proves its savage instincts on the bridge, the radio waves (can you believe it, they banned the Montagnais pop band Kashtui from any air play?) and in the media. Second, Lise Payette, ex Parti Quebecois minister and soap-box queen, makes the film "Disparaitre"—an apocalyptic, revisionist, racist film that clearly posits that the advent of the dark Tamil race into Quebec (to the accompaniment of jungle drums) is going to destroy Quebec (blond child in an out-of-focus wispy shot walks gingerly on a peaceful meadow to the accompaniment of Wagnerian pathos.)

And the film is aired across the country on C.B.C. television. That, sure as hell, triggers in me the desire to "Burn, baby! burn!" But I am cool. So I write a play, *Nobody Gets Laid*.

Uma: The whole metaphor of heat and irritability for instance. . . .

Rana: The summer heat is not just the heat of summer; there's the sexual overtones, there's the whole incest thing, not just between the brother and sister, but it is also about putting four immigrants together in a room (in a place—Quebec—which is hostile to their presence); The Mohawks take up arms in Oka. The entire Canadian establishment, the Quebec media, the army, is reduced to slithering snakes war-hooping around the First Nations, with a blatant racist performance. So we, new communities, do a counter strike. We say—here we are, we are another bunch of "misfits," transplanted aboriginals who will not fit into your great white plans.

Uma: Earlier you spoke about your search for precision and your love of spectacle. Two of your most ambitious sets have been in *Five or Six Characters in Search of Toronto* and *The Sulpician Escarpment*. The former has a confounding array of action on the stage, with live music and strobe lights and fluorescent costumes, street signs etc. but everything worked really well and you pulled it off. In *The Sulpician Escarpment*, you had two brilliant ideas—one of using a Montreal landmark with both historical precision and abstruse symbolism, and the other of having three unrelated men from India stepping off the same plane in Montreal and then tracing interconnections between them. There was so much promise there, the acting was good, there was a measure of suspense and local interest etc. but somehow the play did not succeed; what went wrong? did stagecraft have something to do with it?

Rana: *Escarpment* was going to be our magnum opus! Yes, that's how I felt. Years of experimentation on stage, on introducing filmic elements (I had shot extensive stock on the railway lines in Calcutta and Montreal and had edited them together), the film-noire angle—cobbled streets, gas lamps, the Dashell Hammett figures and with the backdrop of exile politics—voila! we had a murder mystery on top of that. I guess the Escarpment introduced too many edges. The average theatre-goer, and I do not mean it in a derogatory sense, is not prepared for so many disparate elements. There were times when people were. In fact, my plays would fly in New York city. Montreal is caught up in too much of its own separatist angst. The other reason why it did not take off, was because the intensity of relationships between the two main characters sort of got in the way of the progress of the plot.

Uma: What you have said about your early life has helped me, and will help a great many others, appreciate the nuances of *The Sulpician Escarpment.* All your plays demand a lot of work on the part of the spectator/reader, and I have done my homework, as you and others in the field know. But I confess I throw up my hands when it comes to *The Death of Abbie Hoffman*. William Wordsworth wrote his *Preface to the Lyrical Ballads* to educate his generation into reading poetry the way he did. Please don't be as verbose and repetitive as he was, but could you educate me into seeing what you are getting at? Spell it out, please, because I am planning to include that play in a volume that I am editing.

Rana: I admired Abbie as I have admired Lenny Bruce; I say this because Abbie was a symbol of a time, that is now lost forever, no matter what. It was a time of rebel spirit laced with enormous comic-relief about the contrite ways of the Establishment. The passing of Abbie, his "death" to me was the defeat of ideology and the birth of the right-wing trash "common sense" counter revolution. So the larger picture is the ignoble collapse of passionate beliefs in change—that is the death.

But it's all going to come back, in different ways.

Abbie, aside from being written with symbolic disdain for the consensus of triumphant right-ism, is also a reflection of the notion of "point-counterpoint" theory—which means the sharply divided lines of separation are no longer feasible. With the advent of this much used terminology of "globalization," there has come a blurring of lines. Revolutionary zeal can become oppressive. The right can make some intrinsic sense. The enemy can sometimes be very rational. Within a big lie, there is a big truth. Or, simply put, learn from the enemy. So in the larger context, this free flow of knowledge highways has had some mixed impact on politics and the emotions. Chaos and lack of roots are not so bad after all.

Uma: Hey, wait, that rings a bell. That bit about roots is what I say in the title itself of my play, *Rootless but Green are the Boulevard Trees*.

Rana: So maybe you will get what I am saying. I think chaos can bring order. So the "death" has to go from our lives. Abbie, I love him. He was a bend in the road. You know, I got the idea for *Abbie* from Badal Sircar's "Michil" or "Julus" and I kind of readapted it to the 90s. *Abbie* was a refreshing look at everything, a direct attack on hypocrisy, and his death was symbolic of a passing of an age of youthful challenge. So I trashed the right as well as the boringly correct. So it caused some confusion. There you go!

Uma: I have been writing about Serai as part of South Asian Canadian Literature because you are its founder and lead figure, but *Serai* is perhaps to be seen as a voice of the minorities rather than as South Asian Canadian. How do you feel about this?

Rana: Personally, I am a South Asian Canadian. Personally I

will always be an Indian; but I am willing to transform myself into anything else if it would help the cause. But *Serai* the magazine is evolving into the voice of the minority communities as you said; the guy who does the cover for our magazine is Armenian; Lisa is Irish in origin; the guy who is helping us with the layout is Quebecois; Mark Krupa is a multilingual Canadian born in Montreal of Polish origins; Jaspreet is a Sikh chemical engineer from India, who is completing his Ph.D. here; Prasun Lala, who is in *Teesri Duniya's* recent play, is a Bengali born here in Montreal, and part of our original group. One of our young writers is David Austin, a black person who grew up in England. Himmat is our musical giant. He is a gay activist with many years in England. And there is Kiran, of mixed Italian and Gujarati descent. There are the stalwarts—Dolores and Nilambri, Anglo-Indian and Punjabi. So there's a good mix of South Asians and other backgrounds. We are a special blend.

Uma: In many ways, *Serai*, the theatre *Serai*, is like the theatre you grew up with, passionate but unrecognized, with no money but nevertheless active. However, there are the practical realities of financing a repertory theatre. As you say in *On the Double*, when an Englishman has an emotion, he suppresses it; when a Canadian has an emotion, he applies for government funding. Do you think you might ever get funding from any government or community source?

Rana: I am not saying we want funding from South Asians; nor do we want money from the government because we are minorities; we deserve funding because we provide alternative theatre.

Uma: One last question to bring this talk full circle. Given all the trappings of high tech to which you have access, are you satisfied with yourself vis-a-vis-Tapas Sen?

Rana: I will always feel humble before the feats of Tapas Sen in those times. But technically, I believe in zapping the audience—why put them through an hour and a half of entertainment, which they paid for, and let them go without a charge! Therefore, I will always do hi-tech effects. The problem though is dineros! Robert Lapage uses electrical hoists, swings, motors, computerized holograms—obviously *Serai* is still and will be a beggar's opera. But we will give the audience a blast anyway, plus serve thoughts to go home with. The times are bad, Uma. Political content has to be subtextual, but achieved with techno-effects. And form is important. Yes! the medium is the message.

NOTES

1. "Rana Bose and Montreal Serai" in *Toronto South Asian Review*, 7:3 (1989), pp. 37-48.
   "Drumming Toward a Better Future." in *Contemporary Issues in Canadian Drama*, ed Per Brask (Winnipeg: Blizzard, 1995).

Five or Six Characters in Search of Toronto

Stage Notes:

In this production we intend to emphasize not so much the geography of the location but the politics of locations bound by time and so situate the central idea of the play in TIME ZERO. Time Zero is the end of an era, a level playing field, no rules hold, no ideas are sacred, nobody holds sway, there is a back to tribalism element in the way all powers and groups do things, anything can be tried. Time Zero on the other hand could also provide the basis for starting out all over again with a clean slate. Time Zero reflects the poverty of ideals at the present time. Time Zero is also the space in time "where" the west finally won. At least for now. All that has signified the east is on the run. The victory of the west, at time zero, is coincident with the rise of tribal passions—portentous of a primitive future. An inward directed, clan-like, mob decides the turn of events. Division, borders, separations, cleansing—while the facade of free trade is foisted on nations as a panacea. Shades of DOAH!

What are we escaping from? Not Montreal. We are trying to escape from Now. What is Toronto? Toronto is a popular whore, out in time/space. Mecca/Valhalla/Babylon. The 401 is thus a jungle trail, leading to a mythical Cite d'Or.

The Oracle or the Muse interjects to locate the play at time zero, describes it in various ways. The band of six, as a counterfoil to the Oracle, play out his description of a tribal present. Some of the six characters are tribal from the very beginning e.g. the pan fundamentalist. The elements of exclusionariness in the critic, as well as in the PM intellectual, add to the tribalness at a different level.

We must deemphasize the Conference a little and therefore the acronyms (?)

[Staging Notes: This play has been staged in various versions, at Toronto and Montreal. It is best suited to a black box type theatre. In its Montreal version, there was considerable use of light, sound, special effects, cues and live music.]

CHARACTERS

Woman 1: Woman intellectual and academic going to a Toronto Conference. Full of radical and correct theories, totally incomprehensible. Played by Jennifer Chew (Montreal), Nilambri Ghai (Toronto).

Hockey Player: (Hockey Jock). He-man, jock-type, comic relief—motive?—more money in Toronto? Goes from person to person, trying to connect the concept of bricks with the conference acronym and his own hockey lifestyle. Playful, funny, mercenary but ignorant of the "other." Should preferably be fluently bilingual. Played by Mark Krupa.

Woman 2: Quebec Gen-X activist, anti-hippy, who has given up on activism in Quebec, hates boomers. Shift in the wind in Quebec. So she is shifting to Toronto. Played by Samantha Quinn.

Woman 3: Art council critic, litcrit type, writing guru who has abandoned Canada's messy multiculturalism for the businesslike "oneness," south of the border. Twist she is by nature intrigued by orientalist exotica. Snotty, stuck-up, needs sexual action. Played by Lisa Foster.

Man 1: One who carries the brick to Toronto (*Pan-Fundamentalist*) for the laying of a shrine, next to some existing shrine. He is the embodiment of crudeness, cunning and backwardness. Played by Prasun Lala.

Man 2: Aspiring South Asian writer, with big chip about being marginalised. Manipulative, crafty and commercial. Played by Anirban Choudhury.

Lunatic/Oracle Dead Bus driver who comes back as Guitar-man. As they near Toronto, they enter a tunnel. At the end of the tunnel, Toronto should appear. But the tunnel never ends. Actually we find ourselves back in Montreal, in a bus driven by HIM. He drives the bus. He drives the play. He plays the guitar. He lays down the line. Played by Himmat Shinhat.

Directed by Rana Bose.
All music composed and performed by Himmat Shinhat.
Dance choreography by Angela Seth.
Song lyrics by Rana Bose.
Lighting Design by Rana Bose.
Production Manager Lisa Foster.
For permission to produce this play, either as an extract, or in its entirety, please contact Montreal Serai, Box 882, Station "H," Montreal, Quebec, H3G 2M8, Canada.

Scene I

THE BUS CRASH AFTERMATH

Set ideas. As you enter from the lobby, you see signs for Toronto and Highway 401. On a dark stage one can barely see, painted on the flats, the outline of a city at night in the distance. Large pieces of black cloth spread over cubes, squares and rectangles, with white stripes on them which glow only in the dark, like on a highway. The stripes could also be obtained by luminous paint. The luminous tape continues down from the cloth, onto the stage floor and then up one black wall, to produce a distance effect. There is a bench in front, covered by a black cloth with luminous stripes over it also. The cubes, squares and rectangles which are set up with black cloth over them, can be used so that the players can hide under them. When play starts, lights suddenly go off. Ominous electronic sounds float in, mixed in with the sounds of highway traffic. Fog machine has already been on to create a slight haze. In the dark, a man in black steps on to the stage, with a remote mike on reverb mode. In some versions, this portion has been done from backstage, but live. In the background the Bus Driver can be seen, as an electric guitarist, a protagonist and as himself, strumming soft notes, framed by a backlit archway.

Man (Director): (*Under a dim spot*) Toronto. The big T.O. Big city. 6-lane highways. Skydome and CN tower. Jutting into the sky like a second hand Manhattan. Paradise and Mecca. Dream city for some . . . Babylon for others. Toronto—wet, woolly, rude and erect. Fits all urges, fits all desires, full of schemes, full of myths. Toronto ravages the senses and turns on all your headlights, man, (*Two car-like lights come on at the back to frame the guitarist and he starts a process of lurching back and forth to his own very metallic riffs—feed-back and distortion begins*) yes, and that's what it's all about tonight. So far that is, unless you wanna change things around. The rules for the night are clear. We have a highway, that heads west, starting from right here at the Strathearn Theatre, and a motley crew in a bus, right beside you, on this side of the 401. Dislocated, dented and demented. Why? Because the bus to Babylon must crash, my friends. Can I get a crash? (*Guitarist "crashes" on guitar.*) Yes! And after the crash, by the side of the road, there lies the debris—bent, twisted, out of shape. Minds chasing isms in an era without isms. And the haze and the maze continues—controlled by our chief technician Catherine Cahill, sitting right up there in the booth. Fog and lights please! (*Fog and moonrays frame guitarist*) yes! So far things are in control. But who knows? Who really controls these players? Deep down in the recesses of this stage is the man who holds the steering wheel, to another bus, the keys to the highway and the picks to the guitar—(*actor's name*)—the alien and the xeno that gives you the phobia—and you are part of this alien journey, my friends. So, don't play audience, like you do in most anglo plays in this city, and you with the striped shirt . . . yes, you . . . sit up straight, there is a bomb under your seat . . . this bus takes no slack, my friends . . . (*high power techno with guitar work from guitarist. Lights by now have gone off, at the end, real crash sounds happen on the track. Screaming starts, along with fog machine, and slowly blue light appears. Only Man 1 is moving around with startled looks. By now, the black cloth is being worn by Gen-X, Woman Academic and Hockey Jock, wrapped around their bodies. Their faces cannot be seen, as they crawl around very slowly, groaning, on the stage floor. As lights fade in, the haze is visible. Man 1 is seen, panic stricken. He is looking for his brick. He goes from one black heap to another, but nobody shows their faces to the audience, except Gen-X when he lifts up her face suddenly her pancake make-up is startling. He drops her head, startled. Then he bounds into the audience and picks up the brick from under somebody's seat. He is a little comforted, but then sits down with his brick and again breaks into a panic*)

MAN 1 (Brick Man): (*Sits down like he is bawling.*) Bhoiya, yeh to garh marh diya . . . kahan peh, aah geye, yeh? I am fucked! Where is all my people? How am I gonna get to Toronto, with my brick?

Woman 1 (Academic): Excuse me . . . ?

Hockey Jock: (*half under the black cloth, raises his butt first*) Shit! de bus driver!

Man 1: Fuck the Bus driver! The bus driver? Oh! (*Goes over to the ditch, edge of stage [bench], mimes seeing the bus driver's corpse. Hockey Jock brings out his stick and slowly mimes pulling the head of the corpse from under a seat*) But where is the . . . ? (HOCKEY JOCK *bows his head and starts refrain Na Na Na Na, Na Na Na Na, Hey hey Goodbye. Man 1 rocks in a devotional style and ends up saying with dancelike movements—Hare Rama, Hare Krishna, etc. suddenly stops and realises and continues in previous tone of panic.*)

Man 1: Garh mar diya, ekdum, kahan na meiney. I am fucked.

Woman 1: What?

Man 1: Arey, nothing, nothing. you will not understand! Saleh, Aurat hain na! It has something to do with the state of the mind regarding the disruption of your plan of action which is equivalent to being caught unaware, bodily, while preparing for holy congress. You will not understand.

Woman 1: Ah! Well did you say understand? (*Speech style*) If you are talking about representation, or rather the appropriation of Black consciousness, we all agree that one of the biggest problems in the discourse of post-modernism is that it marginalises the black subject . . .

Man 1: What subject . . . object . . . We have to get to Toronto. Let us discuss . . .

Woman 1: Ah! Did you say discourse? Whatever discourse you would like to engage in, must and should be accommodated in a reflexive view of the other . . . and if your concern is that you are being marginalised . . .

Man 1: Margin, what margin? All I said was that we are fucked! Okay? We are fucked. Please, I have to get to Church Street Toronto, if you don't mind . . . must get a ride . . . Taxi! Taxi!

Hockey Jock: You expect a taxi to take you to Toronto, on the 401?-Check le Hindou!

They are all looking at each other. Sometimes cars go by and sometimes they slow down to stop and then take off again, inviting a lot of slang from Hockey Jock.

Woman 3: (*From offstage, then appears on stage*) Excuse me! Has anybody seen my suitcase—a brown leather suitcase? Has anybody . . .

Man 2 (Writer): (*He appears from under a black cloth, while looking at the audience.*) I know that voice. I know that voice. This is the famous . . . my ticket to . . . Aren't you?

Woman 3: Yes, I am . . . I am Ms. B M from the Writers Workshop in Iowa, United States of America, have you seen my brown . . .

Man 2: Brown? Did you say brown. now, let me see. Here we go . . . here . . . which is it . . . (*pulls out paint colour shades from hip pocket.*)

Woman 3: Oh my God. I mean, did you know there were so many shades of brown. Let me see . . .

Man 2: (*to audience*) I am an expert at locating coloured luggage in any part of the world. That is why I will make interesting interventions throughout the play, on such issues . . .

Woman 3: But I have to get to Toronto with my luggage . . .

Hockey Jock: How can you talk about luggage at a time like this. . . . Our bus has crashed . . . The Bus driver is dead . . . (*Man 2 leads Woman 3 to the side saying . . . let me find you what you are missing, madam . . .*) Il est mort! Dead!

Man 1: (*switch to southern preacher accent evangelical*) Dead? There is no problem, there, son. What is death really? Death is just the temporary victory of one tribe over another. (*Switch back to Indian accent.*) It is only a type of temporary transmutation! Like . . . landed Immigration . . . Passing from one body to another. Death is only the beginning . . . Death is only a temporary thing . . . leading onto bigger and better things (*suddenly gets angry*), like smashing churches and building new temples. Death is life giving. For some strange reason, some people insist on clinging onto life, even when they have passed the stage of usefulness. Here, look at me. I am carrying a brick, with a mission to destroy a church that was built hundreds of years ago over my forefathers' dead bodies and we shall not forget their original insult . . .

Hockey Jock: Ah ha! Wait a minute. Haven't I seen you, handing out flyers in the metro? (*sees Woman 2 crawling out from under a black cloth, meaning*) Oh! my god, where is the first aid kit?

Man 1: Who moans there? Friend or foe? What is your tribe, girl?

Woman 2 (Gen-X): (*crawling out from under the black cloth*) Is this Quebec, or am I watching MTV on . . . ? Ohhh! Ahhhh!

Woman 1: (*looking at Woman 2*) The formal relativism implied by post-modernist discourse might have specific resonances for those who have been subjugated to a generational gap in terms of what they have seen, but not experienced.

Woman 2: What rubbish—look, either it is Quebec or it is Ontario.

Man 1: Neither. I think, neither. There are no signs. No English. No French.

Woman 2: No signs in English or French?

Man 1: Maybe then we are already on Gerrard street where the signs are only in Punjabi and Chinese!

Woman 2: I was sniffing into my zip-lock bag and then I fell asleep when the bus crashed, you know . . .

Woman 1: Fell asleep! Well! Interesting hypothesis. Fell asleep, at the hour of decision! No English, No French! Wow! Are you suggesting, maybe we are caught somnambulating while history was being made on the distinct margins of two indistinct solitudes. Question! Could that margin be Gerrard Street?

Man 1: Question! could that margin be Hull? Again she is fucking with the margin! There are no signs here of anything.

Woman 2: Naturally! No surprise! Sign of the times! (*Angrily*) Why do we need signs, anyway? Look buddy, make your choice between pain and drudgery. Head west my friend. Where is your commitment to the new frontier? The hippies are in the White House . . . lots of promises, but no commitment . . .

Woman 1: Commitment? interesting! To what my dear? personal development or social liberation . . . ?

Woman 2: Liberation! Hah! Peace sister! I meant libation. I need a beer. (*Takes out a bottle*) My last bottle of St. Ambroise. Adieu Quebec, Bienvenue Ontario! (*Hockey Jock comes rushing in with fast hockey slide moves, and opens her bottle with his teeth, with great relish, bares his belly, very disgustingly and then leaves. She takes a swig and spits it out. Woman 1 looks at the spit for a while.*)

Woman 1: Ah, I see what you mean. Quebec is going through a phase of entropy, playing god to the rest of the country . . . meanwhile ideology lies devastated, like an emaciated master rat in a sewer full of ninja boomerlettes. (*Hockey Jock leaps onto stage, does several very lightning fast martial arts moves, almost swipes everybody in the process, shrieks, yells, then suddenly subsides and calmly trots out*) Excuse me, who are busy demolishing and deconstructing to pave the way . . .

Woman 2: For revolution X . . . and fuck the boomers. Take it from me. I have lived through this hippie hell!

Man 1: Revolution X! Did she say X! You mean X like in X? That makes sense?

Woman 2: Why does it have to make sense? Does bottled oxygen make sense? Do small Japanese orange trees in your living room make sense? Do the parents of kids who read Roald Dahl make sense?

Hockey Jock: (*reappears from the wings*) I think I found the road. I saw some lights on the other side of the road. Let's check it out.

Man 1: Good! Good! Let's go! Let's go!

Woman 2: What? Across the field? The bus crashed here . . . obviously the road should be near here.

Man 1: May be we slid on the ice. We should take a look . . . Mr. Jock, Mr. Jock! Wait! . . .

Hockey Jock: The name is Jacques, OK?

Man 1: OK. Very good, very good. So Joq, I have a . . . my flashlight (*takes out small pencil light from inside his fly. Military music commences and Man 1 follows Hockey Jock around the stage and copies all his moves, albeit clumsily.*)

Hockey Jock: (*sees the ice*) It's just ahead. Look . . . the ice . . . the ice . . . the tire tracks. I told you we were close. Look . . . (*mesmerised*)

Man 1: OK, OK, but so what. What is next?

Hockey Jock: This is it. This is it. How fate is strange . . .

Man 1: It's the other way round . . . How strange is fate!

Hockey Jock: How fate is strange . . . you, who carries the brick to Toronto, meets me who is born to slide on the ice . . . on this very ice. Look! Look out there . . . what waits at the end of the ice. A shining cup made of pure silver . . . glowing in the bright lights of the big T.O. (*kisses the air*) Hah. They didn't want me in Montreal . . . But Pat Burns! I am your man. Next June the cup will be ours. The spirit of Pat Burns has taken over my soul. It is burning inside me. (*Hockey Jock turns his back to the audience and kneels down. Man 1 stands over him. Light spot on two of them only. Man 1 switches to his southern preacher accent. He has a healing stance.*)

Man 1: Burning spirit! The spirit that burns. You are infected. You are possessed. You are deluded into believing that you are in control. Oh! Your time has come and gone, my son. You've fought your battles and lost and now you must put your faith, your undying faith in me. The time has finally come and its number is zero. I am now in control. I will purge all your rational impulses, all your false visions and tolerant desires. I will purge this burning spirit. I will purge everything. Oust! Oust! In the name of the father, his gun and my parched throat, I declare you dispossessed. (*Slaps him and switches to Indian accent.*) You may now kiss the bride, but not on the lips, hah!

Hockey Jock: Hey wait a minute la! This is going out of control!

Man 1: But what about the road?

Hockey Jock: What road, mon ami? We should take the road of the ancient Indians. There were no roads, no bus drivers then. They followed the path of the buffalo.

Man 1: Bufelo, like in jeans booffelo? Wait a minute. Wait a minute Mr. Hockey Jock. We are back where we started from. (*Pause. Sound track voice says "This is the last time I follow a white man."*)

Woman 1: Excuse me sir. Are you also going to a conference in Toronto?

Hockey Jock: No I am going to the Maple Leafs training camp. But you know, I have seen a Zamboni driver hit by a hockey puck, but I've never seen a dead bus driver. There is no justice. I have a game to play tomorrow.

Woman 1: The banners of justice don't flutter, any more, my friend. The winds of change have died down. What desolation! Look at the faces of the audience. They all have single issues on their minds. The biggest issue this year was the right of white people also to sell smuggled cigarettes. Who is there to call for the overthrow of the whole system . . . (*looking ahead*) Malcolm, where are you when we need you the most?

Woman 2: Hey right on! Radical, man. I was in Oka, in '90, you know. (*Gets up, puts on red headband.*) Yeah! Yeah! You know what I mean, all the starin' and Lasagna and all that, man! Wow, you're not bad for an old hippy you know! So what's next on the agenda . . .

Woman 1: My dear young person! Justice cannot be delivered. It must be snatched away . . . reappropriated . . .

Woman 2: Oh! will you get off your hippy high horse and tell it like it is? We are the ones who have been cleaning up after you guys raised all the high hopes. I mean get real. Quelle fucking drag!

Man 1: Excuse me madam, praise the lord, in my culture we say justice will be served. It is in the forecast on the forehead. Very soon . . . brick by brick . . . Our mission will be accomplished. We must get to Toronto. In Toronto . . . there is hope. Where lies the CN tower, the famous skydome, there is justice. At the conference. By the power of Allah.

Hockey Jock: Are you also going to the conference?

Woman 2: (*Is sitting down*) Yup, something like that. I must, before I am accused of apathy and indifference. I believe that out there you don't really have to make sense and that makes sense to me, and besides it's quelle fucking drag to be tormented by the dilemma of whether at 22, I should live with my parents or crash at the unheated pad on the corner of Mountain and St. Jacques. I mean is this justice? Should an entire generation be hanged and quartered because there was no Vietnam in our time? Are lesser dilemmas any easier to resolve?

Man 1: There is no justice period.

Woman 1: What justice were you talking about, sir . . . what is your mission. Are you going to the same conference I am going to?

Man 1: I am carrying bricks.

Woman 2: No kidding . . .

Man 1: To the West. Yes, that is my mission, to reconquer the old frontier . . . the mysterious and exotic West, where lies Toronto . . . where lies the famous skydome, the CN tower, where LLB or not, you continue to be MP. (*Changes accent*) Sweet Jesus, let me explain this to you in plain and simple language. As long as you believe in the power of your own beliefs, what you see, sweet Jesus, when you close your eyes, is more powerful, more life giving, more divine, more fulfilling, than the trash that you touch or see when you open your eyes, than the blasphemy that you see pouring out of the media, in colleges, or in the works of two-timing heretics turned writers of cheap verses. Let me explain this to you, brothers, and sisters too. The evil empire is finished dead and gone and given birth to unlimited opportunities for all believers to stand up and be counted! Spread the word about the good lord to all his sheep. Whosoever diggeth a pit, will be buried by it. So dig not any further, just skim the surface. Let the lord and the maha-almighty enter into you. The humble servant must carry the brick for his temple and abode. Let the almighty enter into you and you.

Hockey Jock: Bricks . . . ? Are you?

Man 1: Let me stop you right there. I am what I am. Please no prejudgement about my funda . . . It is nobody's business why I am carrying bricks. Nobody has the right to question my mental abilities, which I am sure is on everybody's mind right now, when they so easily, and might add, so academically, (*rushes to Woman 1*) condemn my ability to exercise control over a lot of people, all over the world, at this particular point in time, and this may come as a complete surprise to you, because the very ground that you stand on is very shaky. (*Woman 1 flinches*). Hah~ Hah! And if I may be allowed to continue . . . it is TIMEZERO . . . Construction, deconstruction, inclusion, exclusion, appropriation, reappropriation . . . when you are finally exhausted, you will finally know, why I carry bricks, and what exactly is my holy cause . . .

Hockey Jock: Is that brick dense or is it hollow?

Man 1: Hollow? Hollow? (*furious*) I will have you know . . . (*bangs it down on the floor.*)

Hockey Jock: . . . your head is full of bricks . . .

Man 1: Exactly, bricks are coming from all over the world. Bricks will redeem our lost honour. It is with these bricks that we will right a centuries-old wrong. But first we must break before we build . . .

Woman 1: That is very assertive. Everything you say almost sounds like the truth, except you add so much more to it, that after a while it seems you have a separate agenda, somewhere else. It is like writing your own version of history, with an extraordinary injection of unsubstantiated mythology.

Man 1: Oh! Thank you very much for your compliments, none of which I understand, nor do these people in the audience. But it is nevertheless a good beginning . . .

Woman 3 has come back and is trying desperately all this time to stop passing cars. Woman 2 laughs at her efforts and she finally pretends she's got an idea. Man 1 is curious and in a way egging her on. (Yes! Yes!) She starts peeling off her clothes slowly. One layer at a time.

Woman 1: What exactly is your strategy and what exactly are your tactics? Who are your potential allies and who is your target audience, may I ask?

Hockey Jock: You do this often?

Woman 2: Don't look at me like that. Can't you see, I am trying to hitch a ride to TO. Does it ring a bell?

Man 1: Bell? Temple bell or cow bell? Or Taco bell? It sounds very perceptive and genial. (*Staring at her*)

Woman 2: If this don't work, I will take out my vibrator. . . .

Man 1: That is fundamental. Vibrator? Will it shake us out of our misery? On the other hand, if I do not get a ride I will walk to Toronto with my brick. In the meantime I will rest by the roadside, which is conveniently located along the front row of the audience here, and do some "pooja" like worship . . . (*He sits down in a yogic posture, takes off his jacket and his shirt. Immediately a passing van comes to a screeching halt. Lights fade out. Everybody indicates that a van is stopping for them.*)

All: "A bus has stopped for him."

Man 1 stays with eyes closed. Hockey Jock shouts that the bus has stopped and Woman 2 puts her clothes back on in disgust.

Hockey Jock: Wait a minute, now. Who gets in the bus first? Obviously, whoever can get in first! (*smiles*)

Woman 2: Just a minute, I am the one who stuck the thumb out first . . . I am the one who stepped forward on the highway . . .

Woman 3: You did not. You were not even interested all this time and besides . . . you have no deadlines, no schedules . . . you are in no rush . . . in fact, you were not even sure where you were headed . . . and besides, do you have any references, hah!

Woman 1: Obviously, there is some confusion here about priorities and unless a studied effort is made, we are liable to behave in a most deleterious fashion, which is totally unbecoming . . .

Hockey Jock: I say, each one as per his ability. So, do you know how to make a powerplay, do you know how to use force, when it counts? Can all of you skate on thin ice? have you tested the waters? And most important, have you seen the light . . .

Woman 3: Excuse me, none of you really fulfill the requirements, as outlined in the reverse of this original invitation issued . . . here . . . which says right here that only resident amateurs with known professional standing . . . get that . . . and with several stints on several council juries, can apply to go to the conference. I mean this conference is exclusive and only those with a sense of exclusion can hope to be included.

Man 2: (*climbs up on a cube and spots turn on Man 1 and Man 2* *only*) Inclusion? but inclusion is my birthright! I must get on this van. I cannot go as unaccompanied luggage. How can a face like this be excluded . . . exotic, bewildered, lost, oriental gem . . . waiting to be cuddled, fondled and further mysticised . . . how can I be left alone in the middle of a barely retreating Canadian winter . . . while my sponsor, my ticket to the mecca of publishing, boards the bus, unaware that she is about to meet her match in poetry, fiction and .

Man 1: (*eyes still closed*) Flattery will not get anybody anywhere. On the other hand, blind faith and a mastery over the minds of the masses will. (*Smiles*) It is time when all things that have stood the test of time, must face up to the reality of ZERO. (*Sound track starts—very newage-ish, with percussion*)

All: Zero?

Man 1: Exactly! it is only those who are the heroes of zero, who can emerge from this darkness and come to the light.

Lights fade while music stays.

Scene II

THE ORACLE APPEARS

The ORACLE—Busdriver, Guitarist—appears, stage rear, center, below the arch. Lights are diffused. As he speaks, with wizard-like movements, the music track increases slowly in volume.

Sound Track: Time Zero. The masters of this time are those who have overcome all isms and inhibitions and control the guns that overlook the passes that lead out of the mountains and into the new world. NATO or no NATO.

Oracle: But before there was the New World, there was Mr. C. And Mr. C. crossed the blue sea to reach Haiti, which, on landing, he promptly declared as the Indies.
But alas, as we all know,
It was neither India,

nor was it Toronto,
And as the natives discovered to their chagrin,
the meaning of the words, ringing,
"Go west, young man, while the time is zero"

And in the west, came the pioneers
who eluded all the rest,
and pushed all the way
to the western edge.
The natives almost disappeared,
Except for a few,
who chose to bug the rest,
and sell the cigarettes.

And in the valleys, the canyons and the prairies
grew towns, villages and cities,
while the west went on a picnic
till it had tamed the rest.

And out of the scalping
and the wagon circling
(worldwide that is)

Came the Ford Motor Company
With the model T hierarchy,
And the words that still ring the bell
"Go west, young man, go west"

And now with Columbus dead and gone,
Mr. C that is,
And Taylor, Elvis and Nixon gone,
We chanced upon the pentium chip
in the valley of the silicon.

And amidst the techno hype and techno sin
the Oracle stood up once again,
and muttered the famous words,
"Go west, Bill Gates,
this time
with speed and with haste"

And so with the sun of IBM,
setting in the west,
There is the question
of Mr. Jean Chretien,
and all of the rest.
The brain is in a curfew
The tribes round the bend
The mind is in a freeze
at time point zero.

As the lights switch "tribal" score has already started and a tribal dance choreography happens here—along with a sound tracked verse. All six actors wear white masks with war paint stripes on cheeks. They have a tuxedo painted on their chests, like a bib, their backs are exposed. The lights are arranged to resemble a forest like presence. As the dance ends—fade out—they take off their masks and are found back in their old clothes, in the bus. The Oracle is the driver.

Scene III

WOMAN 3 and MAN 2—IN THE BUS

Only Woman 3 is seen sitting at a window seat. Very composed, reading glasses on her nose. She is reading the New Yorker. *There is nobody else it seems, in this section. There is a gurgling sound that gets more and more pronounced. Man 2 appears from behind one of the seats. He has spotted her. He crawls on the aisles, hops over seats, taking a long time to come closer and closer to her. It is as if he is like a mouse. Finally he settles down on a seat close to her. She is not at all disturbed by him, so far.*

Man 2: The toilet at the back is occupied. Naturally. All toilets on all western expresses are occupied all the time. If you have not completed all your holy ablutions within the first hour, you are treading on dangerous ground. Literally. Pissy territory around the latrine. (*Occasionally sneaks a glance at her.*) That is why one is forced to venture into the front section, where famous writers and critics must be left alone to pursue their just-back-from-seeing-a-friend-in-the-village, leave-me-alone-to-read-my-new-yorker image in holy isolation. (*In mock wonder*) But look at all their faces! Don't famous literary personalities like Mordecai Richler occasionally have a movement? Doesn't Nick Auf der Maur ever feel the need to pass wind? Doesn't Leonard Cohen ever need to use a toilet? Why do these famous personalities always look like they are holding back something? Or maybe they never take a bus? (*Woman 3 shifts in her seat. Man 2 moves a seat closer.*)

Man 2: Now check this out! (*Change accent to regular Canadian*) This is known as forcible occupation of mental space by crude means, albeit, in a moment of temporary isolation. (*Starts reading very audibly from a notebook, switching back to a positively ethnic accent*) Crap, shit, fuck, jerk, jerk-off, hump, bugger, bugger-off. (*Looks at her. She is red in the face.*) Dumb-fucker, bum-fucker, mother-fucker. Every language has its own underground dirty-talk. Coming from India and being stereotypically vegetarian, we have the leguminous varieties, naturally! Huh! potato-fucker, brinjal-fucker, okra-fucker—every language, you see, has its own slime-tongue that hovers around various type of sexual acts illicit or licit? Madam, is there such a word as licit? (*No response. Woman 3 looks at him over her glasses once and then goes back to her magazine.*) No response. Tactic fails. Subject is determined to remain in the isolation chamber.

Man 2: You don't want to hear it, you don't hear it! You don't want it, you don't get it—but if I want it I get it. Ha! Ha! (*Pounds his legs on the floor in mock excitement. He now takes the seat right next to her. She is now a bit disturbed. He stretches out and turns off her light. She turns it on. He turns it off again. She turns it on.*)

Woman 3: Excuse me sir, it is my reading light that you are turning off.

Man 2: Turn-on, turn-off, tune-in, tune-out, be cool, be in, get hip, get down, get funky—no problem, I have full control over all this '60s stuff. You favour which era . . . this that or the other? Personally I am a playwright, personally you are not! Ha! Ha! That is a little bit of irritating Peter Sellers routine that I can never get rid of! Ha, Ha! But I know you are a famous writer, right? Fully funded and subsidized. Personally, I am an ethnic type, fully in tune with all current writing styles . . . but unfortunately, I am ignored, shafted and stereotyped. . . . I am sideline, you are in the mainstream . . . lucky you . . . unlucky me . . . (*sad*)

Woman 3: So, are you a writer sir? In Montreal?

Man 2: You would rather that I am not, right? Stay in my native village in native India, right? And write in my native tongue, on native folklore?

Woman 3: (*Blushes, puts away her magazine and is generally more than curious. She stretches out her legs, in a relaxed fashion, revealing a little bit of leg.*) So do you write in Hindi, Urdu or Poonjab?

Bhangra music breaks out and Man 2 breaks into dancing, very vigorously, through the aisles and then comes back on stage . . . . Finally music track ends.

Man 2: (*Jumps off stage*) In all of the above . . . plus English and French. Surprise? Heh~ Heh~ You obviously did not expect? Naturally. (*Switch to regular Canadian accent*) Now why on earth in the midst of all this English/French mess in the ancient ruins of Hochelaga, would a man from India try to impose his postcolonial heritage in a post modern bus, headed for the west?

Woman 3: (*Raises her eyebrows*) Wow! I mean wow! (*to audience*) Did you hear that? How insanely informed you are sir!

Man 2: (*gets up towards audience, in a different accent*) Just a minute. Did you notice the cryogenic contempt with which she just patronized me? No? But how does it matter? First step . . . heap guilt on WASP critic till she feels stereotypically uninformed, ethnically deprived, and sexually bewildered. Works profoundly.

Woman 3: How totally enthralling! (*She sits with her legs folded on a seat.*)

Man 2: But there is more to come! This is just the beginning. Next comes the aggressive oriental rejected plenipotentiary role. (*Switches back to old accent and gets back on stage. He slowly turns towards her.*) Madam, last time I wrote a book of poems—you pissed on it. You said I violated all the sacred rules of prose and poetry laid down by John Milton to Irving Layton. Now, who made them the yardstick or the reference point? The time before that you came to the release but did not review. You see my eyebrows are rising slowly in a very aggressive fashion. But every time there is a shit-bang short story by some prairie farmer from eastern Europe, who escaped from Stalin, who incidentally is the son-of-a-bitch cobbler who makes the west turn over twenty times, every time his name is mentioned—you make such a fuss about their personal lives that the actual story is never reviewed. And so it goes on! Blah, blah, blah. What about how much we suffer, when we turn on Hockey Night in Canada with Don Cherry and his dog, giving Canadians advice on how to skate around on all issues. (*Hockey Jock stands up to protest, but sits down soon*) Period. And by the way, despite all this TV torture, who's winning all the Governor General's awards? Us or them? You see my nostrils are flaring out in livid anger.

Woman 3: I must do something . . . for you. When is your next book out? Oh! But wait a minute, I am booked for the next several months . . . (*takes out her note book*)

Man 2: A little bit of Arts Council officiousness there, but never mind all these distractions! As you can see it is now working . . . on to the next stage . . . a little bit of outright flattery now, well understood in all cultures! So busy you are. Do you have time for anything else? Do you have any time for us . . . see look at my eyes . . . how simple . . . gentle . . . soft spoken . . . we never get angry even though you stack all the Arts Council juries with your own people. By definition we are calm . . . . see . . . feel my skin . . . does the shade fit the sample . . .

Woman 3: (*gasps*) Oh!

Man 2: (*to audience*) It is working again!

Woman 3: Sir, you must understand, being the only critic for the *Times*, I carry a heavy burden . . . and I really was dumped with this . . .

Man 2: (*During this next passage Woman 3 becomes physically unsettled and restless*) You have a major responsibility! You have to provide support and encouragement to us . . . and I must succeed with my special brand of writing and you must succeed in overcoming your acute liberal dilemma and giving us special plugs. (*To the audience*)

Woman 1: The English speaking milieu is so enthralled with its self-perceived notions of tolerance and pluralist conscience, that it has to adopt us as their ethnic darlings. What choice do they have? Notice how she is undergoing spasms induced by lack of knowledge about the unknown sexual rhythms of the oriental mind.

Woman 3: But sir, I don't know you . . .

Man 2: From Adam! Another anglo-saxon expression that negates the existence of non-biblical civilizations. Why Adam? Why not Sikander? Why not . . .

Woman 3: Pat? Would that be . . .

Man 2: (*To audience*) Now check this one out. It really works. (*With his eyes screwed up in mock disdain. Music is decidedly Indian. Man 2 struts around the stage for a short while.*) You people . . . (*clears throat*) . . . you people (*she is ready to shrivel!*) were wandering around in animal skins, while we had built cities with underground sewer systems. Our code of ethics . . . was talking about pluralism, while you were busy looting and burning. Nobody told you, did they, that Alexander's conquests ended right on the border of India . . . and did they tell you that he was dying of the clap, while your books said he was bored with his conquests? Your history books are full of chapatis . . .

Woman 3: We must meet, Mr.?

Man 2: Mr. Lal Krishna Joshi. B.A. B.F. (*Double*), that is . . . B.A. appeared in the exams two times, but failed two times.

Woman 3: Oh! Don't josh me, I am Ms . . .

Man 2: You are most welcome.

Woman 3: But I did not thank you for anything.

Man 2: Oh! It is in advance . . . that is how we do it back home..

Woman 3: But I did not even tell you my name . . .

Man 2: Oh that is forbidden. I know your name. You are already a woman—I worship the ground you walk on. That is what our religion says. . . . Here you say I scratch yours, you scratch mine. . . . There we say with our eyes . . . thank you and most welcome in advance . . .

Woman 3: You are such a . . .

Man 2: . . . a cross . . . . a cross between Krishna and Axel Rose . . .

Woman 3: What?

Man 2: Exactly . . . (*to the audience. Man 2 moves away from her, in large swirly confident movements, climbing up on different seats . . . throwing glitter as he speaks. Lights change.*) I am a cross between cunning and artlessness . . . between skulduggery and blind faith . . . between guile and orthodoxy. I deceive, make-believe, delude, bluff, bamboozle, circumvent, mystify, conjure, juggle, cheat, plagiarise. (*laughs*) I dupe, doublecross, trick, cajole, flatter, ensnare, lure, decoy, entice and I throw dust in the eyes . . . but also . . . I am committed to the obvious, the veneer, the surface, the ripple at the top, the thinly spread margarine, I speak in godlike undertones (*slowly*) . . . and sometimes I switch on to a Sufi trance and I scream till the zits on my face explode. I scream out, and they love me in my shorts . . . do you know Krishna?

Woman 3: (*By now she has followed his every move and has secured a standing position on another chair, stage right*) Do I know Krishna! And do I know your famous epic the Kamsoot? (*She is bathed in a blue shower light. She seems less stiff. Loosens her hair.*) I know Krishna like I know you, minute by minute more than ever before . . . so bodily, epicurean, sybaritic, pleasureful. . . . I want to be contiguous with you, in this (*she looks around*) first class cabin . . . you sensuous, palpable, tangible, lickable, deluxe oriental cadillac. (*She swirls around and comes closer to him*) I want to graze, scrape, brush, make contact, collide with you. I want to feel, palp, finger, thumb, tap, pat, tickle, pinch, nip, scratch, stroke, lick, tongue, twiddle, fiddle and bruise you. (*She screams it out.*)

Man 2: (*with heavy accent*) I can dig that! let us then lay siege on Toronto, which lies out there somewhere, unsuspecting about our mutual talents. (*Back to the audience, they hold hands . . . music is loud . . . they move to the back of the bus. Blackout.*)

Sound track fades like into an echoing well: Tickle, scratch, nibble, lick etc . . . overlaid with the cast repeatedly saying "Toronto."

Scene IV

ACRONYM DEBATE

In the background, we see the legs of the critic and the writer at the back of the bus. The whole group troops around the seating arrangement in a choreographed fashion, led by Hockey Jock. At the end of one circle . . . they start. Bus driver continues to drive with a secret smile.

Hockey Jock: What kind of conference is this, exactly? What is on the agenda? (*Approaching everybody*) The letter X, safety pins, le vocabulaire complique, le brique, or le hanky-panky?

Woman 1: This is a conference against the intrinsic exclusionism practised by the contemporary Canadian state and the gradual erosion of values. The conference acronym H.U.M.P. stands for . . . for . . . the Hour to fight Un-Canadian Methods and Policies in politics . . .

Woman 2: What kind of hippy/boomer trash is that? . . . Are we going to the same conference or what!

Man 1: Exactly, this comes as a total surprise to me. I was under the impression . . .

Hockey Jock: Oh, wait a minute, time out time out . . . one by one . . . you my dear (*to Woman 2*), first . . .

Woman 2: The conference I am going to . . . and I hope it is not the same one as the rest of you are going to . . . has the acronym H.U.M.P. (*The writer and critic suddenly jump out of*

their chairs at the back, and slowly come to the front, straightening their clothes and hair). HUMP stands for Hell Unleashed on Madras shirt People . . .

Man 1: Madras shirt People? Madras? Like in Madras?

Hockey Jock: Oh! ben oui! The Madras shirt is an old hippy thing, Tie-dye, batik, Jerry Garcia, eh?

Woman 2: And the Ontario government has finally woken up to the facts of life . . . they are determined to stand up against . . . this 60s trash . . . spend, spend, spend! Jesus! This baby boomer berkeley tribe must go . . .

Man 2: Sixties? . . . like in the sixties? . . . Be-Eatles, Free Love, Peace brother . . . that kind of thing?

Woman 2: Yes, yes. (*Excitedly*) Trash eh?

Man 1: (*Climbs up on chair*) Just a minute . . . Kindly sirs and madams, I believe . . . Mr. Hockey-Jock-from-Quebec, every body was going to get a chance to explain. Why am I being ignored? Do I look like a minority, as is the case in my own country?

Hockey Jock: Le communate culturelle . . . ah yes, they are a visible pain . . . but we can reach our goals without their vote . . . go to with your brick . . .

Man 1: (*clears throat*) Let me clear the air and my throat. The conference I am going to . . . is a kar seva . . . kar seva . . . holy ritual . . . OK? Many hundred years ago, the main mahant of the main temple in the Six Nations Territory from Bufellow to what is now Toronto, had a dream . . . more like a vision . . . and this is long before all this white people, NDP, FenDP appeared on the scene. Long long ago, before everything else . . . before even there was religion . . . and the exact spot where the Lord appeared . . . has finally been determined . . . to be exactly on Church Street, where the Tamil Presbyterian Mangalam Church is now standing. For five hundred years we have waited with patience, for things to change. We went to our brothers and sisters in the native community . . . they will not trade brick for felt . . . we went to the RCMP man . . . they only do "gidyap, gidyap" and ride around on horses on busy streets . . .

Hockey Jock: That is very true . . . that is why we want the SQ to take over . . .

Man 1: Continuing further without any interruptions to our five hundred year history in this country . . . the time has now come . . . we have collected bricks from all over the world . . . all over and we are going to Toronto, Ontario to break down this ugly church, which has remained an insult to our religion for five hundred years . . . and brick by brick, we will tear it down and build our own temple.

Woman 2: So what's the acronym, man, for your conference?

Man 1: H.U.M.P . . . just like yours . . . . Hindu Untarians Mandhata Parishad . . . H for Hindu, U for Untario . . .

Woman 1: U for Ontario! . . . what distortion . . . What a travesty!

Woman 2: Well why not? Who said Ontario had to be spelt with an O? And why do you have to define. . . . Who cares anyway, for your definitions?

Hockey Jock: You mean that HUMP of yours is a . . . like . . . a (*to Woman 1*) post . . . (*to Woman 2*) transcemental thing. It's something that . . . even though all of you are so different. It brings you together . . . like a religion . . . only without the preacher . . . (*verbal diarrohea commences hoping to arouse Woman 2's interest*) You know, I always imagined that there exists something out there that holds everything together. (*Very pensive*) Comment que j'pourrais dire ca . . . comme une force psychic, a power play, an understanding . . . (*struggling, then bursts out*) Dat's it! H.U.M.P.—de Hapocalyptic Unconsciousness Mystical Power play. It's stronger than science . . . in fact it is anti-science . . . it can't be explained in terms of numbers. Like a feeling in your loins, eh like . . . its an H.U.M.P (*spell*) feeling. (*Looks at everyone*) You can't deny that we all share the universal urge to thunder merge!

Woman 2: The what?

Hockey Jock: (*still enthusiastic*) The other day I was watching Shirley . . . they were talking about the invisible HUMP. Like your aura . . . it's there, but you can't see it. The collective unconscious with the archetype, Kirilian photography, spontaneous regression, these are part of HUMP. It's simple. Some people like each other; some don't, some are Leos, some are Scorpios. (*To the audience*) Did you ever get the feeling of being watched by a third party, a non-existent existence? Huh? (*Looks suspiciously at the driver. Sound track is vaguely like twilight zone.*) . . . now that is HUMP, estie! (*grabs his hockey stick with resolution.*)

Woman 2: Hockey is HUMP?

Hockey Jock: Ben oui! Because life is like a hockey game . . . (*At this point, Woman 2 cannot bear it any longer*)

Hockey Jock: *(Continuing*) . . . everybody knows . . . dat dere are only two possible outcomes in a hockey game . . . one . . . you can win . . . (*Man 1 counts on his fingers*) two . . . you can lose . . . and three you can tie. (*Man 1 is confused*) But every game is different because of de HUMP challenge. (*With nostalgia*) I have known a few girls in my life . . . oke, but I know wit yu it's special, because of dat powerful feeling yu give me. I like you . . . you like me . . . but most of all . . . (*running after Man 1*) I want to touch your brique.

Man 1: Hey attention (*French accent*) . . . some French I do know . . . No touch my brick!

Man 2: What is all this crap? (*Who wrote the script?*) Are we going to Toronto or not?

All stand up

Woman 3: Look we are in a tunnel. (*Spot with a gobo, from top and moonstar, with the fog machine.*)

Man 1: Jesus, mother of Murphy~ The 401 has become a tunnel? Jai Ram Ji! But by the looks of the leaks in the ceiling, it looks more like the Ville-Marie tunnel . . .

Woman 3: Why is it getting so dark?

Woman 1: It's an illusion, reality is . . .

Woman 2: Oh! Shut up! Are we going to Toronto or not?

Hockey Jock: We must get to Toronto, estie. Who is this bus-driver!

Bus Driver: Tera Bap Hun Mein! Your father, that is.

All: What!

Bus Driver: Why should you go Toronto? (*In French, as well*)

Woman 3: Wait a minute, is that Poonjab . . . ?

Woman 1: Actually it is a very south shore dialect . . . like from

Brossard..

Man 1: Look I've had it, (*throws his brick into the audience—turns out, the brick is made of sponge.*) First, the bus crashes. Then comes a second bus, and it is driven by a non-Hindu, from Brossard, who speaks four languages. Enough is Enough. The whole nation is being taken over by minorities. What about our rights? (*Ready to get off*)

Man 2: This is a new twist in the plot. This is a distortion which amounts to blasphemy. Let's burn the books and kill the writer.

Man 1: Sala, garh mar diya!

Bus Driver: Sit down. (*In English*)

Hockey Jock: Bilingue, tabernac!

Woman 2: Who are you?

All: Yes, who are you?

Radio announcement—on the sound track, signifying we are in Quebec and that all services to Toronto are cancelled because Toronto does not exist. All look at each other. Bus driver mimes, bringing bus to a halt, turns off engine, gets up.

Bus Driver: I am the Bus Driver. I wrote the script.

Hockey Jock: I have a game to play . . . I have my future . . .

Bus Driver: Stop playing games (*in French*).

Man 1: I have a temple to build with bricks . . .

Bus Driver: Your bricks are killing people..

Man 2: I have an idea . . .

Bus Driver: Your ideas don't work anymore . . .

Woman 3: I am . . .

Bus Driver: That's the problem with you. You can't think beyond yourself . . .

Woman 2: I gotta go to an NDP rave on Bathurst, man!

Bus Driver: (*laughs*) Stay where you are, kid, the raves here. . . . (*Bus Driver heads to the back.*)

All: But we must get to Toronto!

Bus Driver: There is no such thing as Toronto!

All: No Toronto! (*They say "No Toronto," with their backs to the audience, put on shades and the sound track starts. Fog machines on. Before doing the song, the first starting tracks are played and Bus Driver goes to the back, and picks up his* *guitar, the rest spread and the audience should catch the same silhouette as in the first scene . . . then Bus Driver comes forward. Hip hop style song "Who dat alien?" ends the play.*)

SONG: I'm the lunatic
The refugee
I'm the alien
And the freak
(*He's the alien,
he's the freak*)

(Hey de busdriver
surprise us all)

But most of all I'm the driver
I shift the gears
I call the shots
I turn the wheels
(He's in charge
He'll steal the brick)

Excuse me sir,
My time is dear,
I'm the Rasta
I'm the Sikh
I steal the job, You can't keep
(Check it out,
goddammit
He is the freak)

I am the xeno
that gives you the
phobia
I am the devil
from Tasmania
I'm the homeless
the shoe-shine boy
When the job is done
I stomp on your docs
I pee on your socks

(OOh! Disgusting!
He's the compression
that gives me depression
Check it out, he's the one
that's changed the nation)

My mother says to me
all a de time
(Boy, move the
posterior.
Get a vocation)
Give me a tip, mother
Don't be farcical
Speak with words
That's practical
(He's the lunatic
The refugee
The shoe-shine boy
And the freak)
To be effective
To be bonafide
Don't be so
Tight & so uppity

Cross the line
And give up the fight?
(I'm leaving,
I'm running)

I'm the driver
The lunatic
Check out the
abstract
Give me the beat
(Give him the beat,
the lunatic)
I'm the driver
The lunatic
Check out the abstract

Give me the beat
(Give him the beat,
the lunatic)

(Stay where you are
And fight the beast
Stay where you are
And fight the beast
Fuck the 401
Pitch the brick
(Stay where you are
and fight the beast)

Things go in cycles
Before they get
drastic
It's the nineties, they
say
You act like you
know
And you don't do
nothing
(Act like you know
and you don't do
nothing)
Eat, drink,
And live in a zoo
And whine all the time
like winnie the pooh,
(Act like you know
And you don't do
nothing)

I'm the lunatic
The refugee
I'm the power
In the House.

Nobody Gets Laid

The play begins suddenly a few minutes before schedule. House lights fade out and immediately a sequenced rap/metal style sound track comes. It is the instrumental version of the song "Blood on the Barricades." On an overhead slide screen quick slides change of a young boy and girl, like a brother and sister, in an Indian setting. The music is harsh. The slides are soft. Immediately a guitarist is scene live, down stage right, playing very metallic riffs. A woman dancer, cartwheels in. She dances a mix of hip-hop, jazz and pseudo Indian style, to the music. The music, red gels, the dancing is intended as a "hot" beginning to set the pace for the rest of the show. As dance fades out, slide screen is lifted out by a pulley arrangement. Scene 1 begins immediately.

SCENE 1

Lights fade in on a dining table area. In stage left a man, Samir, is sleeping, shirtless, on a chair, legs up on another chair. There is the sound of distant thunder—as lightning flashes through a window on stage right—a woman, Rina, is seen intermittently looking at the man from inside a room for a while. Suddenly, a downpour starts, man wakes up and rushes to the window—lights brighten—woman is gone.

Samir: (*Stretches*) Joi Ma Kali! (*Puts on a shirt*)—Rina, eh Rina—let's have some tea. About time it rained and cooled off the joint. Rina! Where are you? (*goes towards the door*)

Rina: (*She wears ankle bells. Walks out from another door, si-*

lently behind him) Are your friends coming tonight? (*He is surprised by her movement*)

Samir: Of course! Tonight's the big night. No Soccer on T.V.—the whole gang arrives. Jimmy's bringing in lots of taramasalata. (*Her head is a bit down*)

Rina: I don't like (*sigh, gap*) . . . . I don't like that that taratara stuff—and also that greek wine that makes the whole room smell like kerosene oil. (*She sits at the card table*)

Samir: It's not taratara, Rina. It's taramasalata—it's like caviar salad. Caviar for the working class of Park Extension. I like it!

Rina: It is a pink caviar. Working class colours that are faded and jaded, not the real stuff.

Samir: (*Silence*) I don't understand you—why don't you work somewhere else—like in a library or insurance office or something—I mean I had very little schooling—you have so many degrees—MA, BA—and what not.

Rina: They are of no use here.

Samir: But why in a bloody sweat shop (*sits down with his tea*). I don't understand. Is this why you wanted to come here from all the way in India? You know—sometimes I wonder about you. You had so much over there—and here you are a slave in a stocking factory. . . . Nobody even knows who you are. Why did you want to come here. I mean is this all you want to do? (*He waits for a while.*) Nothing else? You know, you could go back to University. Rina, I would do anything for you. (*She swings around and looks at him. The door bell rings.*)

Rina: The rain has stopped, its gonna heat up again. (*She leaves. He opens the door. Mrs. T. enters. Large woman, with Irish accent, wears jacket and a workman's belt.*)

T: Fucking heat!

Samir: Fucking heat is right man. Tell me about it. Let me get your jacket.

T: Uh-uh (*Walks over to a stool and sits down. Pause*) Fixed the sink in the floor below. Good thing you ain't living below this lady 'cos the water ran thru' the walls, man. Fucking heat. Makes your hormones simmer, eh Samir? Until the rains come along and everybody's relaxed and the rain feels good!

Samir: Not here for me, here the rain don't have it for me.

T: Only for a while, Samir! It cools you off.

Samir: Fucking rain comes and goes like there's a quota system. You know like—street by street—here and there like a lawn sprinkler. Gone! And the heat is back on.

T: Not like your India! The rain eh!

Samir: (*making tea*) Hell no! Hey Mrs. T! Back home rain is like a water cannon from 10 feet away! (*mimes*) Non-stop for 3 days till only big tall fellows can get out and swim with the dogs and the shit. Check this out man—This is Montreal—supposed to be cold—and here we are.

T: Sweltering in the heat. Yes. The heat is on buddy,—sign of the times. (*Wipes her brows*) Sign of the times. There's gonna be a lot of sweating around here. And here we are not dealing with it head on. (*Opens a can of beer*)

Samir: What's that mean?

T: What that means? Ha! It means, the heat is like a curtain. It's out there—covering something. Beyond the curtain is another set-up. You know. Right now nobody's put their cards on the deck. You don't know and I can't tell, Samir. Nobody wants to pull the curtain aside.

Samir: Quebec's getting hot eh! I know what you mean. But it's still below the surface. Not like when we first came here, eh? This time . . . (*gives her beer. Pause*)

T: This time Quebec's getting hot, Samir—hot for a lot of people—not for itself, but for a lot of people.

Samir: (*silence*) You mean for . . . us.

T: (*interrupts*) I mean. . . . get the door, there's somebody dying to get in.

Samir: How do you know? (*Samir is a bit surprised. Goes and opens the door. Enter Jimmy the Greek with a big container of Taramasalata.*) Tikanas! Taramasalata—caviar for the working drunks of Park Extension.

Jimmy: Heh! Check it out man—I make it myself! No much junk eh! Only the good stuff. Not like Caverne Grecque or something.

Samir: You mean lots of eggs eh! Pink eggs eh!

Jimmy: Eh, where's you sister man? You know the other day—I see her, what her name, Rini, in Beaubien.

Samir: Rina, yeah!

Jimmy: She just walk away without say hi! She don't like me or what? Hey, you tell her Jimmy the Greek—eh, I be nice to all people—say Hi to all—especially her—she is . . .

Samir: Don't worry about her! She is just very quiet—you know—reserved.

Jimmy: She's very quiet—very cold, numb. No talk eh!

T: No talk! Just 'cos she's not interested in a mediterranean motherfucker, doesn't mean she is numb ok. No talk!

Jimmy: Hey, Hey slow down ok! Mrs. T, don't drive off the deep cliff so easy. Nobody gonna pull you back!

Mrs. T: (*wipes her sweat*) Goddamm heat.

Jimmy: Yeah. You, Samir, get yourself a fan—big fans for sale at Pascal. You know, the turning kind! eh?

Samir: No fans ok? The heat will be gone soon and the room will have less space if I get a fan. After two months, where will I put it?

Jimmy: (*Jimmy lays the table out for cards*) put it in the locker in the basement.

Samir: I got no locker, fool.

Jimmy: Then put it under the bed or you got no bed you stupid immigrant!

Samir: Never mind! We've done without a fan for so long—we don't need a fan now—besides you gotta get used to this heat in Quebec—it's nothing.

Lights start fading out on all except spot on T.

T: A fan is a good idea, Samir. You not gonna get used to this heat. (*Pause*) It's gonna be a long summer. Everybody needs to cool off!

A jingle of ankle bells is heard. Rina walks in, towards Samir. Jimmy gets up in the dark to look at her.

Samir: I didn't know you were working tonight.
Rina: I'm not.
Samir: Then where are you going now? It's (*looks at his watch*)
Rina: (*after a while, comes close to Samir*) I'm going out for some air . . . Samir, these card games that your friends play. . . . every night
Samir: You hate them . . .
Rina: . . . . I think they are invasive . . . they take over, Samir . . . they drag you away. . . .
Samir: Where. . . . where will you go now . . . It's kind of late.
Rina: . . . . These card games. . . . they are debilitating . . . do you know what that means? (*Samir shakes his head*) It means . . . (*a little smile*) they are incursive . . . yes? No? it means they get in the way . . . maybe your friends are right. . . . you need a fan.
Samir: How can you start . . .
Rina: . . . . And if you don't get a fan, there will be no resolution . . . the heat is going to get worse . . . and the air will be thicker . . . . people are gonna gasp for air and then they will be at each other's necks.
Samir: Rina! (*She leaves. Lights off*)

SCENE 2

Radio DJ belts out weather report in the dark (Radio station is called C-HOT) and then spins "Blood on the Barricades" a rap-bhangra summer beat. Station plays globe style music. Lights fade in. Card game is in full session. Manuel, Terrance, Ali and Jimmy around the dining table. Samir is seated on a bar-stool, chewing on an apple. Jimmy is more drunk than the rest.

Manuel: Turn off the radio, man—turn it off.

Samir goes over slowly. As he approaches the radio—it shuts off itself. He stops and smiles. When he steps back, it starts again. Everybody smiles hesitatingly.

Manuel: (*In Spanish*) What you doing? Some kind of witchcraft or what. Hey check him out.

Samir steps forward and the radio shuts off again. Ali gets up to take a better view. Terrance slaps him down.

Terrance: Me say you play the game or go play with Samir, Ras.
Manuel: Tabernoche! This place give me the creeps everyday. Yesterday, I was in the toilet and when I pull the flush . . .
Terrance: Shut up man, it's yuh turn, ras.

Manuel mumbles to a stop. They settle down to a few seconds more of card playing. Samir goes over and shuts the radio. Walks back to the stool. There is silence for a while. The lights fade to a glow on the card table. Rina is seen watching Samir from inside the room. They play cards for a while. Card language proceeds. Rina goes away.

Samir: Fucking heat! Like a curtain—or something like Mrs. T says.
Ali: In Teheran, we buy fans if it gets too hot. Before it was Indian fans imported from Rossiya. But nowadays we buy Korean fans from Germany.
Jimmy: In Athens too we have Indian fans on the ceiling, turning.
Terrance: Yeah, Sam, what's your problem Man. Me say why you dont go and buy a fan.
Jimmy: Yeah, from Pascal!
Terrance: Yeah from Pascal, Ras, so these guys wud shut the fuck up and play the game.
Manuel: Maybe the fan would be possessed like the radio and start moving around on the floor. (*Ha! Ha! All laugh*).
Samir: Look guys, OK, Look here and listen to me carefully. . . . I won't buy a fan . . . no fans in the house ok? No fans! You wanna play cards, you play cards. You want the breeze on your face, go to the lakeshore, OK? No fans in this place.
Jimmy: What you got against fans? Man, I don't understand. Or is it 'cos your Quebecois girlfriend will cut your throat off, if

you buy the fan? Hah! How come she mother you so much?

Ali: (*playing his turn*): Yeah, what's the matter Sam? You let a white woman run your life? You Indian hero—Raj Kapoor! He makes the girls run around him!

Samir: Shut up Ali— Shut the fuck up ok! It's my apartment!

Jimmy: Eh wait a minute, wait a minute. It's his business too. (*Stands up*). We can go play cards anywhere we want to—you the one who make us come here—if it's not nice and comfortable—why we play here? Eh, Terry? Besides your sister, that Rini, she don't say hi to me never.

Samir: I don't believe this. (*Repeats. Stands up*) For the past several weeks, we don't play a single deck nice and easy, like we used to—every week it's going down the hill man! If it's not the heat, it's Bourassa, if it ain't Bourassa, it's my sister, if it ain't her, it's back to the heat.

Jimmy: If it's the heat, its gotta be the fan. (*Samir cuts him off with a loud scream.*)

Samir: Shut the fuck up.

Manuel: It's the heat senor—it's the heat. (*Bell rings.*)

Jimmy: She here—she gonna cut your balls off, if you talk about getting a fan. (*Samir lunges for Jimmy's balls. Jimmy doubles over in mock pain. Samir opens the door. Marie-Helene walks in.*)

MH: Bonjou Tout'l monde.—I can hear you guys from outside. (*Everybody greets her. Jimmy gets up and takes a big swig.*) I'm not gonna cut his balls off (*to Jimmy*) if he buys a fan. But I might cut his head off.

She pours herself a drink and comes and sits on the bar stool with Samir. They embrace.

Terrance: Yeh, Marie. We decide we are gonna buy a fan (*in French*). (*He winks.*)

MH: (*en francais*) Now don't start the evening off with the fan business, ok! I told you people, you don't need a fan. It's not hot here, OK!

Manuel: No it's not OK! Why shouldn't we have a fan? Tell me why does all talk about the fan drive you mad? eh? What you say Terry? Is heat embarassing? (*All laugh a little*)

MH: (*a little unsure—en francais*) What do you mean by that?

Jimmy: He means the heat is for real—eh—like a curtain—it stick to your body—it's not something you can deny—it's all over, it's not . . .

Manuel: He means it's not something you can hide—it's not something you put in your pocket—outta sight outta mind.

Ali: He means, it's real—objective reality—it's not metaphysical or something.

Terrance: Yeah man, objective for sure. One of us is going to keel over pretty soon with the Iranian's pit odour—6 card run (*lays out a section of his card on the table*). Here!

Manuel: Fuck. I was wondering who had the seven of spades. It's the heat. It's playing games with my memory.

Marie: (*en francais*) Again! You know, you guys come here and then you want to fuck with the weather. This is Quebec—OK—you can't change the weather here—I've lived in this city for 28 years. The heat comes and goes like that. 15 days maybe. After that what's he gonna do with the fan? Hang it up in his closet?

Jimmy: He gonna pack it up or put in the kitchen window backways so all the turmeric smell go out into the neighbourhood! Ha!

MH: (*Goes up to Samir*) Are you planning to buy one?

Samir: Settle down, honey—I haven't made up my mind.

MH: Well what's gonna make you make up your mind.

Terrance: He's gonna make up his mind himself—cos he don't need your help for that, Marie:

Manuel: (*To Ali*) Don't fucking look at my hand!

Jimmy: You know what's a problem, Marie? I tell you what it is—to you whatever you've heard, is what you want to know and whatever you know, the whole world around you must buy and if they don't buy it they are a bunch of fucking immigrants who are fucking with the weather changing the rules—ok?! You play hockey, we like soccer—let's keep it that way, ok?

Terrance: Eh! Jimmy—what's you problem man—settle down.

Jimmy: Fucking heat! I gotta right to complain about the heat—

my wife's complaining, my kids are complaining at school—everybody's complaining about the heat! And she say there's no heat. Just like that. Why? 'Cos it's Quebec? So they no heat?

Ali: Jimmy, what she means, is the heat is no big deal—you got to get used to it.

Manuel: But first we got to agree there is heat. If we all agree there is heat, then we do what we gotta do to get used to it . . .

MH: What do you take me to be . . . some fool with my eyes shut. You think I don't know Quebec is changing. . . . I'm saying it's easier to adjust . . .

Jimmy: I tell you Sam, if you don't do something about the heat in this place—I'm leaving, OK! I'm leaving—no more card games here ok! Next time . . . (*Rini enters the room. The little bells on her ankles can be barely heard. Everybody falls silent and watches her as she glides across the room and goes inside.*) (*After some silence*) Phew! Next time we play in the pool room on St. Viateur.

MH: (*to Samir*) Samir, how come she is like that—amazing how she silences everybody without a word—just the way she moves.

Samir: She's in her own world—she needs to be away from all this (*agitated*)

MH: Ever since she . . .

Samir: (*interrupts*) Now don't say ever since she's been here, things are going wrong . . . the heat and all that . . .

MH: That's what you said dear . . . not me.

Samir: I said . . . she needs her own place . . .

MH: Then why does she hang around you . . .

Samir: (*Shrugs*) Like you . . . you hang around me . . . (*smiles*)

MH: I hang around you . . . because

Samir: Parce-que. . . . Why do you hang around me?

MH: (*en francais*) Because I like . . . I like Indians who like to drink english tea . . . and talk with a parisian accent (*moves closer*) . . . You're such a strange bird . . . Samir . . .

Samir: So now I'm a strange bird. Fucking heat's gotten to you too. . . . You beginning to sound like a CBC special about the exotic orient . . . tea is incidentally of Chinese origin . . . not english.

MH: Well, I like Indians who drink Chinese tea and speak with a Parisian accent.

T: (*Appears at a certain height—slow fade in. She is on some kind of a ladder working on a wall. Rest of scene fades to a glow*) Some people like the fucking heat, some people deny it, some people know how to deal with it, some people don't —I tell you what, the heat's been simmerin' underneath for years. The heat is nothing new. Marie-Helene is right—people got to get used to it, but she is wrong to deny that it exists. (*gap*) You wondering why I'm telling you all this . . . Me? hell I dont give a damn. Everybody, here is fucking each other and nobody is getting laid . . . and that includes Judeo-Christians. (*Lights fade out.*)

SCENE 3

Rina at stage right. Standing. Light spot comes on her very slowly. There is a gentle sound track at the back. Not mysterious, but serene. T appears on stage right, working on a chair, under a spot. The bar from the previous scene can be turned around on wheels and with proper lights can be made to look like the cavernous entrance to a hut, with a thatched roof.

Rina: About twenty years ago, in an obscure, sand-swept village in Northwest India, I was playing an old game with five stones and pebbles, with my brother, Samir. Samir invariably attempted to bypass the rules of the game. I had just slapped him for making another such attempt and then as in a ritual, I was holding him close to my heart, as he wept incessantly. As his weeping died out, I could hear in the distance, the growing sound of a mob coming closer to us. A crowd of shrieking men and women were coming down the only village road. They looked furious and uncontrollable. I suddenly realised that they were headed for our hut. I grabbed Samir's hands and we rushed to our hut. We made it before they did. There were men and women who were shouting about witchcraft, demons, voodoo and animal rituals. One woman was continuously wailing as she carried a live chicken in her hands. At first they stood outside and railed and ranted. They were fearsome and getting uglier by the moment. The village chief had also joined them.

My aunt, who looked after us, had just given birth to a child, the day before. She sat motionless on the floor. The child was gently sucking at her breast. The crowd was relentless. They hurled abuse at her. Called her a witch. My aunt's husband had died four years ago. She had stood her ground. When she got pregnant, very few people knew. She was a small woman—with a lot of energy. When she smiled, her eyes seemed to dance. She was a brave woman, who did just what she pleased. Nothing could stop her. The villagers were determined to have her blood this time. With the husband dead four years ago, she could only have been sleeping with Satan.

T: Ah Satan! You don't sleep with Satan. There is no passion there—there is only grief and when there is no passion we are all in trouble, my friend.

Rina: They finally shored up all their spineless group wrath and entered our hut. My aunt sat still and stared back at them. For a moment there was silence. Then the woman with the chicken, leapt out of the crowd, ripped off the chicken's head with her bare hands and started flinging the blood in all directions. The shrieking was interminable. Our pots and cooking utensils were being thrown all over the room. The clay oven got a massive kick from the headman and it rolled on its side. The blood was on the walls.

The shouting continued for a while. My aunt with her child sat still on the floor. After a while, the passionless cowardly bunch, ran out of things to fling. They slowly backed out of the hut, all the while shrieking and hissing at my aunt. As they slowly moved away—Samir hugged me and started sobbing gently. I went over to my aunt—she sat still with her baby. I saw her face and I knew, this mob had, for the first time, dented her soul. (*pause*)

Next morning, the village well was choked with the bodies of my aunt and the baby. 10,000 years of primal energy had been contained and sublimated by a pre-Victorian village well.

T: Now, if she had killed instead, she would go down in history as a witch, a senseless witch—with no sense of the mood of the times, but instead she bowed down to them, she gave in to them and changed the course of history, permanently.

Rina: Samir grew up in the dusty haze. As he grew up, he grew apart—an excellent soccer player who raced around my life, rippling with energy. I admired him. I went to the city, to do my BA. He never finished school, but started working as an apprentice in a machine shop. I lived in a hostel in the city. Samir lived in another city. I cared for him. But I could not hold him close to my heart any longer. There was something dark about my caring for him. I could not frame it. When he hurt his ankle in a game, all our girl cousins from the city came over to look after him. He lay stretched out on a reclining chair. They gently turned him over. One of them ran their fingers through his hair. He was in pain and needed care. I stood away at a distance and stared at him. He was oblivious to the care I wished to give him. My brother. As I close my eyes, I can see him lying on the chair. He left India for Canada as an engine room technician on a large tanker. I never got to see him. He was gone. My obsession for him remained. I was his fan forever.

SCENE 4

Lights off. Radio DJ is heard, talking about the heat, Mohawk/SQ stand off at OKA, etc. Finally turns on a song—fade out. Lights fade in on stage left. Samir and Marie-Helene sit facing each other close on two bar stools. The stools are back to back. A lot of the exchange between the two is in French. The argument between the two starts out pleasant, playful, gets a bit hot and then again settles down.

MH: Because?

Samir: Because?

MH: Because why! Tell me?

Samir: Because it's uncomfortable . . . it is . . .

MH: It is what . . .

Samir: Look, you're sweating . . . look in your armpits . . .

MH: I have glands Sam, I sweat . . . what do you have, by the way.

Samir: I have glands too, but I treat them right.

MH: Ah ha! You treat them right! Does every Indian have a fan under his glands? Are there enough fans as there are glands? I mean . . . c'mon Samir!

Samir: MH, if a fan can . . . never mind. Let's settle down now OK!

MH: I know what I'm talking about, OK.

Samir: But, you don't know what I'm talking about. I don't want a fan, cos it's gonna please Jimmy. OK (*he shouts*) It's the whole group, it's the whole group . . . they figure they want a fan . . . they can't put them fingers on it . . . they feel something's going wrong OK? . . . I don't want a fan to cool off myself or the others . . . but if a fan is what . . .

MH: A fan is not gonna do shit! OK? Listen to me! You have to get used to it! They've been playing for months! Why suddenly now?

Samir: Because there was no heat then! Now it's hot. HOT! Hot everyday, hot every night . . . every night . . . I can't sleep . . . I feel something's wrong, you know . . . every night they fight . . . It's not like before . . .

MH: Samir it not like before, because before . . . last summer . . .

Samir: What about last summer?

MH: Who was here last summer?

Samir: The same gang.

MH: (*walks away*) Uh-uh. Think about it, not the same gang.

Samir: What do you mean not the same gang. What're you talking about?

MH: Last summer

Samir: Last summer . . . we didn't feel the heat . . .

MH: Last summer . . .

Samir: Things were more laid back . . .

MH: Last summer .

Samir: It was not necessary . . . because the building next door was not built . . . the wind came through right?

MH: Samir! Last summer, . . . you're not listening . . . the heat was . . . not important for you. Last summer, the five of you had just gotten together. The heat was in the street, in the newspaper, on TV . . . somebody else, . . . Somebody else's problem . . . the heat was outside . . . for others . . . OK! Now . . .

Samir: Now, it's our problem . . . it's our problem . . . (*gap*) Yeah . . . I know what you mean. The heat was outside. Now they've discovered us.

MH: (*Waits for a while—like she is composing her mind*) The heat is inside now Sam: It's inside your house. (*They both slowly look at each other. She comes over to him*) But you'll get used to it . . . come closer . . . you'll get over it.

They embrace sitting on the bar stool. They kiss slowly. Rina is seen at the back. Samir notices her and jumps out of the chair.

Samir: Rini! Hey Rini (*rushes after her inside the room*)

MH: Stupid! Stupid! (*en francais*) (*Lights cross fade to card table. MH settles down on the bar stool—head down on the backrest.*)

Terrance: My ass! My ass! Ras . . . is that how they teach you to play blackjack in Greece.

Jimmy: That's right . . .

Terry and Jimmy have an argument over the rules of the game. Details needed. They are all a bit drunk. Ends up with Ali saying—Well, this is how you gonna play it in Quebec! Ok!

Jimmy: Oh! Yeah—you can shove it—(*knocks Ali's deck on the ground. Ali grabs him by the collar. Jimmy slaps him. Ali grabs him. They are on the floor in no time. Manuel goes to a corner and starts mumbling in Spanish. Very abusive. Ali in Hungarian. Jimmy in Greek. Lights flicker. Terrance gets up* *and tries to separate them. The shouting is furious. Ali picks up a bottle to hit Jimmy on the head. Terrrance grabs it. T appears stage left*)

T: Hey, Hey, Hey. Bunch of stupid immigres! Next thing you know Lise Payettes gonna do a film on refugees practising karate in basements. Fucking heat! When you think it's gone, it comes back again like a curtain eh! (*wipes forehead with a kerchief*) When you guys gonna learn. You, Ali, what's your problem? Ain't nobody fighting for nothing these days! Get off your ass Jimmy! (*She walks away towards stage right. MH suddenly wakes up to say something. Mrs. T whips around.*)

MH: Now just a minute . . .

T: Now, you don't fuck with me—'cos I've never fucked with you! (*Both back off slowly. . . . Music starts faintly*)

Ali: Shit! I'm gone . . . I'm gone, man . . . I don't know why I'm here . . . I don't know. (*He leaves from the wings his voice can be heard, shouting loudly in Persian.*)

SCENE 5

Card game in a lull. Manuel is playing patience. Samir has replaced Ali. Terrance has his eyes closed, as radio plays a very slow solo alto sax. As the tune fades out, DJ says "That was our program for this segment . . . ladies and gentlemen it's 2 in the morning July 10, 1990 in Montreal. The standoff continues at Kanasatake. Reads section from CBC news quoting Brian Mulroney. "The demands of the Mohawks are absurd. . . . (laughs) I'll catch you tomorrow 7 p.m. sharp . . . meanwhile keep your cool . . . the temperature is rising."

Samir starts back. Manuel goes over and shuts the radio as it fades. Comes back trying to imitate the sax in a horrible nasal fashion. Terry's eyes open. Irritated.

Terrance: Me got a terrible temper, Manuel . . . me say you don't press yuh luck no fadder, Man.

Manuel keeps blowing the sax and making funny body movements

Terrance: (*stands up*) Manuel . . . me gonna keep muh cool, dis' time (*takes a deep breath*) . . . but yuh listen . . . man . . . when a man feel rotten . . . (*Manuel stops to listen*) . . . when a man feel rotten . . . feel like yuh have nottin left to do . . . you feel helpless . . . feel like the big man gonna ketch yuh . . . dis time . . . like all dis years of fighten and keeping the peace . . . man . . . alonasudden me feel like nottin left inside . . . me feel rotten and helpless . . .

Jimmy: Why you feel rotten, Terry?

Terrance: Dem block di food and medicine for dem Mohawk. (*Repeat in French. Empeche pas la nourriture et le medicament d'entrer*) You don't block food man, . . . me feel helpless . . . sometimes you haffi do sometings . . . weh yuh really used to just to survive ras . . . so now notin you can do from here . . . ok . . . jus no point—johnny got no ratchet, no mon . . . so's me bear the sax comin' thru . . . me feel a lickle better . . . yeah? me figat de present man . . . me feel bettuh . . . de sax is smooth, ras . . . (*gap*) then this chili con carne mudder fucker come and do his mariachi shit. Fucking mexican!

Manuel: Eh Senor! Many times I've told you I'm not Mexicano, OK? I'm from . . .

Jimmy: From Chile . . . capital city is Santiago . . . eh, they sell fans there?

Manuel: They make fans there senor, ok?

Jimmy: Son um a gun . . . we better import one Chilean fan from Chile . . .

Samir: Turning kind, eh Jimmy? Turning kind.

Terrance gets away from the group, swearing & scowling quietly.

Jimmy: yeh turning kind—eh Jamaica man, it's your turn . . . what's the matter . . . the heat getting to you?

Samir: Ain't no heat in this room ok . . . cut out this heat talk OK . . . he's taking a break.

Jimmy: Cut out the heat? Just like that? Cut out the heat? You begin to talk like you boss . . . that Marie-Helene-la.

Samir: Shut up Jimmy—ok—yer fucking obsessed with the heat. . . .

Jimmy: Everybody is obsessed man . . . you obsessed, Marie-Helene is obsessed . . . Rini is obsessed.

Samir: What do you mean that Rina is obsessed?

Jimmy: You'll see . . .

Samir: Don't fucking talk in riddles ok? (*grabs Jim*)

Jimmy: It's the heat, Samir ok . . . it's got everybody obsessed . . . in Quebec, in the street, in the park, inside the house . . . the heat is driving everybody bananas . . . Rini is no exception Man.

Samir: Don't keep bringing her up ok.

Jimmy: She don't say hi to me never—why?

Terrance: Me say yuh obsessed with her . . .

Jimmy: (*silence*) . . . Maybe . . . I think she is . . .

Man: I think she is very beautiful (*repeats in Spanish*) Oh! You very lucky Samir to have hermana like her.

Jimmy: But she got something else in her mind . . .

Samir: Shut up Samir. . . . Keep shut ok and keep her outa this.

Jimmy: Jesus! I can't talk about the heat! I can't talk about Rini—what's the matter with this place . . . (*walks a little distance walks back*) . . . fuck you all . . . when you get a fan ok—call me back—ok . . . get a fucking fan ok . . . get a fan (*puts on his jacket*) Cool this place down.

Rini enters. All fall silent. She walks across to the inside of the apartment.

Jimmy: . . . fucking heat . . . no more Jimmy the Greek gonna come here . . . no more (*he leaves*)

Samir: (*goes after him*) . . . Hey Jimmy, don't leave man . . . don't leave . . . I'll do something.

Jimmy: Get the fan, Samir . . . I tell you get the fan . . . it's not the heat . . . (*their voices fade out*)

Terrance: Me feel de winds changes and go away. Like Dylan say long time back. Times-a-changing—but dis time ita changing other way . . . in reverse.

Manuel: (*Sits down on the edge of stage*) Maybe it's good

Terry—the world is comfortable it seems without ideals, without commitments, without goals . . . it's like it was all there . . . underneath . . . now the real instincts of men show up . . . a little bit of money and confidence and all the hatred, the shit from the sewers have come up on the streets . . . everybody's showing them true colors.

Terrance: Yuh man—people don wanna live together if yuh don't have the same color, same god, same language you start fightn . . . fightn till it becomes too hot to live . . .

Manuel: Yeah . . . but like she, she's not involved in all this.

Terrance: Who?

Manuel: (*whispers*) Rini

Terrance: yeah she got separate world, ras.

Manuel nods his head slowly.
Theme tune starts up—lights fade.

SCENE 6

As theme tune fades out, lights fade in. T is seen trying to fix a chair. She is humming to herself. Rina's bells are heard. She slowly turns around. She is smiling and coming towards her. Behind, the hut glows.

T: Hi Rina—the boys want the chair fixed. One of these days . . . at the rate they are going at each other . . . they are gonna bash these chairs on their heads, instead of sitting on them.

Rina: Tell me, what's getting them so worked up?

T: They're gonna tell you it's the heat, maybe I will too . . .

Rina: But you don't really think it is? Do you?

T: Well, maybe (*gap*) the heat is the times, Rina, it's the times. Everything is hazy, no solutions, just a lot of intensity—but no one's getting it on, you know.

Rina: Maybe the heat is just an excuse for all that we can't express . . .

T: Yeah, it kind of builds up . . . makes you uncomfortable, sweat right? You don't wanna admit . . .

Rina: Yes, and you're not sure what's right, what's wrong.

T: What's moral, what's immoral! People don't wanna talk about it clearly! What's below the surface and what's not . . . They're all feeling the heat . . . and the Mohawks . . . for sure they've caught the whole country, with their pants down!

Rina: There are lots of things people don't talk about . . . they don't question, they don't want to get deeper into . . . and that makes everything simmer underneath . . . it's like nobody wants to clear the air.

T: The times are like that. . . I keep telling the boys, if you can't put your finger on it, don't keep talking about it . . .

Rina: (*She wanders off to a corner*) It's funny . . . there used to be a guy in our village . . . many years ago Sukhdev—his name means the lord of happiness—but he was always worried. He was the first guy to have an autocratic wrist watch in the village—you know the kind you have to keep wearing at night so it moves and won't stop.

T: Yeah, yeah I know . . . I had one Seiko like that . . . .

Rina: Well, we didn't know that that's what it took to make it run. Sukhdev was very secretive. He wouldn't tell anybody. Suddenly, he would shake his wrist during a conversation . . . or he'd pass by someone's hut and suddenly stop and wriggle his wrist. The villagers were terrified by this. Sukhdev would be there on a hill top—in a silhouette at dawn. Steady. Then suddenly his wrist would swivel around . . . and everyone in the village would sigh and say "That's another spell. Sukhdev's got magic in his wrist. Don't let him do that in front of your hut." Nobody questioned him. Nobody wanted to talk about it. Everyone decided it was not to be discussed. Sukhdev's automatic wristwatch. If you asked too many questions, if you delved too deep . . . he would cast a spell, so everybody just shut up. Talking about the times (*she smiles*) He froze us in time with his wrist watch . . . the first automatic in the village.

T: Anybody ever got to the bottom of this . . . I mean . . . did he get away with . . .

Rina: No! No! Not at all!

Rina: Yeah! There was something religious . . . or no . . . something very catholic about it . . . it was like you don't question it . . . like it was direct from god . . . it was the way things ought to be . . . you don't question such stuff . . . the power of the first automatic wrist watch in the village.

T: Amazing!

Rina: Not really! 30 years ago in Quebec you didn't question a lot of stuff . . . if you did . . . everybody would jump on you.

T: Yeah, the church just about had a stock answer and final say on everything.

Rina: And you think it's changed now?

T: Yeah, it changed kind of, but then it's back again through the back door . . . now in a funny sort of way.

Rina: Like how?

T: Oh! Lots of stuff . . . there's a new church in power. . . . I mean who are you fooling? . . . anyway. So what happened to the wrist watch guy?

Rina: Oh! Sukhdev.

T: Yeah! the lord of happiness.

Rina: Oh, he flourished for a while, while all of us simmered in the heat. Then my aunt put a stop to it.

T: Your aunt?

Rina: Yeah! She knew his number all along . . . So one day she grabbed our wind up alarm clock . . . Big one . . . She tied it up with some hemp rope around her wrist . . . and marched off to Sukhdev's hut . . . The villagers followed her from a little distance. My aunt stood in front of Sukhdev's door, turned on the alarm to the clock and shook her wrist violently for a few minutes.

T: (*laughing*) I don't believe this . . . the lord of happiness must have been pissed off!

Rina: Pissed off! He was so shaken . . . and my aunt kept shaking her wrist, the people at the back started roaring, the alarm kept going on. Sukhdev was in a corner crouched (*the lights flicker sound track of people, loud clock alarms*).

T: The bubble was burst.

Rina: My aunt kept shaking her wrist till the big clock was ready to come off her wrist (*the sound continues and she is laugh-*

ing) she was having a great time!

T: It was like an overthrow right!

Rina: It was like somebody had thrown big blocks of ice on a bush fire. Sukhdev's grip on time had been lost.

T: The heat was gone eh!

Rina: Everyone was shaking their wrists—like they had always known.

T: (*laughs*) My man, Sukhdev . . . he must have fled? No? (*Sound track fades out*).

Rina: No! No! Sukhdev stayed. . . . My aunt held him by the hand, brought him out and explained to all of us, why he shook his wrist . . . it was to make the watch work, it was the natural thing to do . . . there was relief . . . everybody felt cooler . . . they felt better.

T: Like the pressure was off . . .

Rina: People were talking to each other . . . there was no secret . . . it was a natural thing to do . . . like you could do what you felt and not feel pressure you know . . . and Samir was there right next to me, smiling away . . . you know we all agreed it was the natural thing to do (*She has a steady gaze*).

M-H enters the room slowly. . . . Rina sees her and comes out of her gaze and walks away. M-H looks at her going in.

M-H: What was that all about?

T: She is intense man . . . she is something else . . . oh! What'd you ask? What was that all about? . . . it's about the heat, mon cherie . . . the heat . . . (*she laughs*) . . . (*Lights off.*)

SCENE 7

Music starts in the dark. Solo song with a pounding drum background. Slowly lights fade in on card table. They seem to be putting the cards down to the beat almost. Tension is evident. Music is tense. Only three are playing now—Samir, Terry and Manuel. Cross fade to sharp spot on another zone. Stage right. Rina is wetting her face with water from a bowl. Her eyes are closed. She does it for a while. Then she takes a comb, wets it and starts combing her hair back till it's wet and slick. She stops. The music suddenly stops. Blackout. A phone rings. Red telephone, immediately picked up by M-H on stage right under sharp spot. She converses with Terrance. Terrance on stage left, real laid back.

MH: Hullo!

Terrance: Hmmm! Bonjour M-H! etc

M-H: So, how come you are not here?

Terrance: Good question!

M-H: What do you mean! (*angrily*) Good question!

Terrance: It means, so far, me not too excited! But yuh barometer is goin up.

M-H: So?

Terrance: So yuh shuda know bettuh.

M-H: What that supposed to mean?

Terrance: It means, for the first time in many months Terrance gonna stay home, ras and make some roti and dal for meself and then me gonna lie down on muh hidabed and stretch delimbs a bit and then me gonna turn on the TV and stare at de worried face of ms barbra frum . . . hey tell me Marie, why she look so worried all a de time . . . and why she got dem square shoulders like a vulture?

M-H: I don't know . . . and I don't care. . . . I want to know why you're not here!

Terrance: Lemme finish M-H, me also think dat barbra frum wear bermuda shorts under dem designer dresses . . . but no one knows dis dark secret (*Starts laughing*) . . . did yuh know dat?

M-H: You're drunk!

Terrance: Sure me drunk! me fix a mean rum wid a chaser and me nice and smashed like true island nigger—lazy, useless and cravin to be home—and you wan me over one more time so we can fuck each other more and more and more and more till alonasudden deh noone left. Dis deh call incest, sistuh! Incest! You fuck each other weary till no one home . . . all leave . . . there nottin to fight for no more . . .

M-H: (*She looks around and notices Rina, barely visible in her zone*)(*Angrily*) So you not gonna come anymore?

Terrance: If yuh keep talkin to me like this, maybe me take a scissor and snip off de cable on me line . . . and dere be peace forever between yuh and me..

M-H: Terry, why are you acting like this . . . Sam's gonna be real upset, if you don't come . . . What's the matter with you? I mean what's all this bullshit? So we're all a bit tired of all this arguing? You think I enjoy it? I'm just tired the way you guys keep goin on the heat! Merde!

Terrance: Tell me, M-H, me luv you woman, cos yuh smart . . . is de heat de real problem? is dat a wat we fighten about . . . or we no put de finger on de real problems . . . me tell Jean-Paul today in de factory . . . why we gotta have a Quebec position on everything. Me say new welfare bill no good . . . he say . . . so go to Ontario . . . why you stay in Quebec . . . me say, 14 grand not gudenuff for Antony Griffin mudder . . . the judge is crazy . . . he say go to Ontario . . . dont pick on Quebec . . . ina everthing he see de national question . . . so we fuck each other alla detime . . . till me feel beat . . . marie-helene

M-H: (*Very unsettled*) I dont wanna hear this anymore . . . I just dont wanna hear this anymore . . . OK? I . . . I . . . (*turns around towards Rina*) hate this fucking situation! . . . I dont wanna talk about it anymore . . .

Terrance: (*gap*) Yeah, me neither . . . say bye to Samir . . . salud—(*sound of phone hanging up*).

M-H puts the phone down. Bright spot on Rina. M-H stares at her for a while. Anger in her eyes. Goes slowly upto her.

M-H: What is it that you want? eh? What is it? (*en Francais*) What is it that is bothering you so much? Why don't you speak? Why don't you say something? What is it that you want from us? From your brother? What do you want? (*Samir gets up from the card table*) Don't you see we are trying to make something out of this? And you are not helping one damn bit!

Samir: Marie leave her alone (*en francais. He comes close to her. They hold each other. Lights fade out. . . . Music.*)

SCENE 8

Manuel alone, playing with a deck of card. Radio on (News etc. play). When radio starts playing a particular song (Sister, Sister)—played later again at the end of the play, Manuel starts strumming chords on guitar with radio song. After a couple of bars—Samir enters—walks to the radio and abruptly shuts it off. Manuel hesitates—keeps strumming. Manuel takes up the song. Samir is disturbed by the song. They look at each other.

Manuel: Amigo, she loves you!
Samir: (*looks up to him*) I know—
Manuel: No you don't amigo!
Samir: Eh! Manolo I know—but she doesn't understand—we are falling apart like a box of cards. Marie-Helene thinks we don't care—that we are insensitive to their needs—we know what language and culture is for a nation, but like Mrs. T says, the agenda has changed—it's not language anymore—it's color, it's race, it's closing doors to children, it's fixing the deck, it's carving up the place before it's too late, it's the economic pie . . .
Manuel: I'm not talking about Marie-Helene. (*He starts strumming his guitar—very dramatic chords. Samir is a bit stunned. Manuel works up the strumming and then stops*) It's Rina, amigo—your sister I'm talking about.
Samir: (*stunned—pin-drop silence for a while. Looks at Manuel*) You . . .
Manuel: You gonna call me a latin son-of-a-bitch?
Samir. No—I can't lose you—everybody's left (*gap*)—But what do I do . . .?
Manuel: You don't do nothing, you just talk to her—at least you have a friend in her—look how we fuck each other and lose everybody—because we can't cut a deal with the heat eh, so

we stay at home and fuck each other all day, all night. We don't go out—we stay at home eh? Now if you ask me I'd say that is incest . . . (*Manuel begins to leave*) . . .

Samir: Manuel, don't leave man, we gotta do something together—bring the guys back.

Manuel: Maybe—

Samir: Maybe ask them again . . . .

Manuel: Ask them what's the real problem . . . talk to them (*silence*)

Samir: Maybe we shall buy it . . . maybe we need it—maybe the more we hide from it we are not gonna face the facts. . . .

Manuel: You think it's gonna draw the line?

Samir: Some gonna leave, some gonna stay.

Manuel: But at least—we will have drawn the line. We will have said—we need this and we're gonna have it—no matter where we live.

Samir: We are too busy feeling guilty you know, we're too busy thinking we will offend somebody, we're too busy thinking what we do is not Quebecois. . . .

Manuel: Meanwhile, we can't meet our needs—we can't satisfy our own passion. Amigo, sometimes we gotta sit back—take stock—what have we had done all these years in the old country? Here we played along with very superficial ideas—ideas like the one that make the mob burn flags, throw bricks, fix quotas for kids in schools—We don't deal with the powers, we just screw with each other . . . eh? You agree.

Samir: (*Pours a drink—Finishes it in one swig.*) Let's go buy a fan! (*Music track—Rina comes into the room.*)

Manuel: No! You stay, I'll go look for a good buy . . . (*Manuel leaves. Samir hesitates, then sits down on a chair facing the audience. Rina comes from the back . . . slowly runs her hands thru his hair . . . there is a sensation of lights—intense glare.*)

Rina: I'm glad you didn't leave. I'm glad we are finding innocence where it belongs—and one is not found guilty when one is condemned—I hope the heat bares it all and we can all find passion wherever it comes naturally and we don't suppress it till it becomes unbearable (*she walks stage front to* *the music*) I hope we live for the simplest truths and by god, we fight for them—because that's the way we used to be before. I hope we can react to the most uncomplicated dreams and not get handcuffed to the mob. . . . Samir, I love you like a sister loves a brother . . . (*lights off—music fade*)

SCENE 9

Lot of commotion generated by Manuel and Samir. They carefully carry in a crate containing the fan. It is a bright magic-like box on four legs. It has a hole with streamers covering it. Manuel's personality has visibly evolved. He looks tough, sounds tough.

Samir: Watch the corner—Watch it, watch it Man.
Manuel: Eh Senor! You beginning to sound like my grandfather! Watch this! Watch that! Put that here! Put that there! What's the matter with you?
Samir: Watch it now! Move this way—now—-Carefully here . .
Manuel: Why there? . . . You gonna put the fan there near the window, what's the point? . . . Bring it back here, no?
Samir: No not there, here! . . . No No little bit to the right.

They finally put it down—near stage center.

Manuel: Eh, amigo, this fan is so big—gonna blow this whole fuckin place away . . . like you see the movie Zabriskie point? eh? in the end boom—everything come down slow motion from the sky—broken arms, dolls, raw meat, coca cola cans, marilyn monroe's lips, tables, chairs, McDonald's signs, everything . . . blow-up everything . . .
Samir: Manuel, your making this sound like a stick of dynamite . . . all we need to do is cool the joint . . . not blow it up . . . tabernac!
Manuel: Same thing, tabernac . . . we've been sitting on our asses, can't make a simple decision . . . for ourselves, 'cos

we're worried sick . . . you need a fan, you go get a fan, you need a stick of dynamite, you go get a stick of dynamite. . . .

Samir: What's the matter with you . . .

Manuel: What's the matter with me? . . . Nothing's the matter with me. . . . We've been sitting here like ass-holes trying to find out how not to offend our hosts . . . in the meantime they've been reaming our asses, heaping guilt on us . . . eh? . . . something wrong with what I said? Tell me . . . something wrong? . . . (*grabs Samir's jacket lapels*)

Samir: . . . all we had to do was to go out and get the frigging fan, and we were sitting out here weighing the pros and cons, the ifs and the buts, should we should we not . . . and steaming in the heat all along. . . .

Samir: What that gotta do with all this? What you talking about?

Manuel: . . . Samir . . . we gotta do what we gotto do, no matter where we are in the world. Nobody is gonna give us permission to draw the line . . . Bourassa, Parizeau, Lucien Bouchard, the SQ, les forces Canadiennes! They will never give permission to us . . . and we have to do what we have to do to make this land comfortable for us. ok? (*Changes expression . . . walks away*) . . . Huh! Look at that box . . . Sitting there . . . the room looks different . . . gonna change the place . . . we don't need no one's permission for that . . . it's gonna level things.

Samir: It's just to cool the joint down . . . cool the guys off . . . ok? Don't make a big case out of nothing.

Manuel: It's gonna cool the guys—cool the room, cool off the city, cool the whole fucking world—(*in Spanish*).

Samir: Good! Let's go to St. Viateur—pick the guys up . . . tell 'em we got the frigging fan . . . bring back the caviar—we gonna play cards till kingdom come . . . let's go let's go . . . (*They leave amidst a lot of commotion. As they leave lights fade and only one spot on crate. Very sharp. A percussion track is barely heard. M-H enters the room in a circular motion, watching the crate from a distance. She prowls the stage restless for a while.*)

M-H: (*A lot en Francais*) (*She looks slowly at the crate*) I guess there's another solitude . . . (*Rina slowly walks in. M-H no-*

tices her suddenly, but does not react immediately) . . . no matter what, it will be separate . . . but they could have waited . . . they could have just waited . . . because the times would change . . . Quebec does not stay hot for too long . . . only a few months . . . it just needs its own place under the sun established . . . first . . . and if you don't let her do that now, it will get diffused with other realities . . . this fan . . . it's a cop-out . . . it's giving in . . . it's failing to adjust to the land that's given you shelter, the land you have come to live in . . . the fan is an intrusion . . . it's a private deal . . . it's fucking immoral, it's giving license to sin, it's giving in to temporary passions (*her anger now starts building, as she starts looking at Rina*) You can't bring in something, that is not meant to be. You can't do whatever you want to do here. You can't bring in your shit here . . . we have our moral codes here . . . it does not jive with yours . . . don't you understand, don't you fucking understand? . . . with every little cop out like this, we will cease to be ourselves . . . we will disappear . . . we will just not be around as a people . . . we will just disappear . . . then you will be fucking happy . . . with your fucking fan (*she kicks the crate. Rina rushes to grab it before it topples over. She holds on to it. M-H starts backing out of the stage*) . . . There is no heat . . . here . . . it's in your mind . . . (*music [last theme tune] has slowly drifted in*).

SCENE 10

Rina drags a chair over near the front of the crate. She loosens her hair. Turns on a switch and cool air starts coming out of the hole that was covered with the streamers. Almost simultaneously, three or four industrial fans, placed strategically, around the audience, are also turned on. They have streamers on the protective shield, which flutter onto the audience. Cards come floating down from the ceiling. Music builds. Lights glow out on Rina.

SCENE 11

This scene cross fades in with the previous scene. As the theme song develops faintly, Rina is seen slowly opening up the crate. There is a sensuousness in the way she moves. The heat is still there. As she uncrates, a while translucent plastic screen is seen billowing at the back. Over and above the faint theme tune can be heard shouts of confrontation between the Mohawks and the Army. A high power search light travels the plastic sheet. Silhouetted forms are seen nose-to-nose in confrontation. Reverb overdubs, playback Oka sounds. Lights criss-cross. Barbed wire. Drum sounds. Finally the theme tune gains. The search lights fade. Only Rina is left. She gradually puts the fan center stage, plugs it on. As she does that, there is a sense of coolness on stage. Only spot on her. The audience must feel the breeze. There is a cool blue tinge, almost like a haze. Feels like a thousand fans are turning. She sits down on a chair, with her profile to the audience. Her legs stretched out, hair in the wind.

Just as the tune is about to fade and the lights go out on her, we see a split second image of all 4 players, at the table, playing intently.

Some Dogs

SCENE 1

Lights dim. Actor, who was conversing with members of the audience, comes on to stage easy and casual—rearranging some of the props and talking to the audience. Brings in a fire hydrant and puts it on one side—rearranges some cubes. Stage has bright panels in pastels. One structure indicates the facade of a two-storey structure with a window.

ACTOR 1 (Kalpesh): (*A little underlying agitation*) I was just telling a bunch of my friends out there—how hard it's getting to do plays in Montreal. I mean, by the way, tonight's play is about dogs—eh—big doggies (*puts down hydrant*)—hey! Anyway, like I was telling them out there, it's getting really difficult—kind of crucial to understand where theatre is really headed right? I mean, you know—we are here on the stage under wraps—you know—under pressure—on the defensive—working our butts off to do a good job—you paid for it now, you want a good return. We want a good review. Now we have to worry about the publicity. Can we pay off the rental costs? Are we gonna have a full house all nights? Is Pat Donnelly here tonight? If she is here, will she write a review? Will she file her review in time? Will Gary Steckles put it in? Will it be in on Thursday, so we get an audience for the weekend? All these are genuine concerns, you know. We have to do all this, plus act and make sure you don't just walk off to a corner cafe after the play and tear us to pieces—"Shit, what was it all about? Now that big lady—

Hey!—now she was superb, but the play—it had no substance—just a series of images. So anarchist." I mean we are under wraps, under covers, you are not—we face an audience that is far more informed than before and even silently hostile. I mean I bet most of you have heard of Bertolt Brecht, epic theatre, living theatre—maybe you have even heard of Dario Fo, Augusto Boal, Fugard—shit, you are all pretty good critics now—regular theatre goers and we, look at us now. We are under the microscope here on stage—plus mind you—we have to run scramble and try to catch Tommy Schnurmacher's attention—Tommy Schnurmacher. Will Tommy say a word for us, now come to think of it—nothing has changed—absolutely nothing. (*Actress 1 walks in from the alley and moves up stage front.*) So from the times of Greek tragedy where aristocrats on stage played down to the plebians in the darkness—there is a role reversal that has taken place. We are now a bunch of goldfish swimming around in an aquarium under an electric bulb and you are sitting there watching us and there is a

SCENE 2

Two unemployed youth—sound track—sound of car pulling up (lights)—one man draws the corpse in by holding around the armpits (feet dragging), drops it and splits (car sound taking off). Followed by "you can't always get what you want" (live band) . . . . Youth 1 sits down with styrofoam coffee cup and stares at it for a while. Youth 2 keeps mumbling the song. Actress 2 is curled up in one corner, barely visible.

Bernie: Jay, Hey! Hey! Do that once again, man, remember (*smokes incessantly*) last time we were here, you did it, man, I can remember the lines . . . the poem.

Jay: What?

Bernie: You know that one about smokestacks, semi's rolling by—man—like the whole world was flying by and leaving behind . . .

Jay & Bernie (together): . . . the two of us.

Jay: Yeah . . .

Actress 2 stands up and comes over to look

Bernie: Do it man, oh con—shit—feels kinda crazy here tonight. (*Gap*) Go on! Go on! (*Pokes and shoves 1*). Man! Remember that time in Jimmy's loft—jesus, you were up there on the ledge—4 in the morning—"cold sheet glass on back" . . . and the fucking cops were coming in their cruisers one after the other . . . shit . . . (*mimics sirens*) . . . and you were up there on the ledge.

Jay: Yeah—(*Stands up and walks across the stage twice—Actress 2 stares at him. Silence for a while. When Jay starts, she gets up slowly and stares at him. Sharp spot on Jay. Actress 2 stares out in the distance—and hums to a tune before Jay starts—piano cords and drums*)

(There was) "Cold sheet glass on back,
looking out at madness,
She rolls down 44, (*Gap*)
Bi-state, semis,
Smokestack two,
In grey-belt deep sky,
Schoolboys in school bus,
Yellow.
Nurse white, red lip doctor
Styrofoam coffee
Spilled on green rug,
Styrofoam coffee, spilled on green rug
(*Gap—looks down*)
I'm not gonna jump off you jerks,
But the damage is done! (*Sits down*)

Bernie: Damage done! Shit yeah, damage done, you know—Shit! Can I have some of that coffee? Can I have some of that coffee? (*Lights spread*)

Actress 1 gets up on the corner and mimes cleaning a table and pouring coffee from a jug and waiting for a "great coffee" response she slumps down on hearing it's "awful coffee"

Jay: It's awful.
Bernie: I have awful coffee all day, Jay.
Jay: O.K.
Bernie: (*Sip, sip*) You remind me of your mother, Jay.
Jay: You don't know her.
Bernie: Yes I do, in fact, your legs are shaped just like hers.
Jay: (*Looks at his legs*) O.K.
Bernie: So?
Jay: So?

Silence for a while

Bernie: So, what's you . . . I mean, why'd you bring me here, what are you, I mean, what are you looking for here? Why are we here tonight for?
Jay: Mr. Goodwin.
Bernie: Who?
Jay: He was supposed to meet me here. Looking for Mr. Goodwin.
Bernie: Oh! Yeah, I read that book.
Jay: It's not a book—and that was Goodbar.
Bernie: Oh! So what's, I mean, what, what's, I mean who's Goodwin. Fuck. (*Gets up agitated*) You gonna tell me something—or do I have to squeeze every word out of you?
Jay: He's got something set up, he says I could do. Give me back my coffee.
Bernie: It's finished. (*Bernie stares at Jay*) Shit! I'll get you coffee. (*Looks for change*) Man! I had some change here, fuck. I must have dropped it. (*Goes around looking for the change and mumbling*) Goddamit, everytime I wanna buy coffee—I got no change and I got no change 'cos Molly's been going through my pockets—it's true! It's true all the time and anyway—I haven't been making any for weeks now (*Gap—walks away to another corner*) You know Jay, I wanna buy a

skimobile—you know—the stuff Bombardier makes—make some money, buy skidoo and go blazing through the snow man—you know. Just go far away—drift into the whiteness—a little black spot getting smaller and smaller while the snow drifts slowly from side to side—you know, man, I haven't worked for months, what weeks. I keep telling they guys . . . I need some work. (*Repeat*)

Actress 2 looks far away—sadness, settles down in sitting position

Jay: Huh! You wanna find work eh? Can't get what you want . . .
Bernie: "You can't always get what you want. But if you try sometime, you might find, you get what you need . . . " So what's Goodwin, Goodbar got set up for you man? What's his hook?
Jay: Bodies, . . .

Woman 2 jerks up

Bernie: What?
Jay: Bodies . . . stiffs.
Bernie: What? (*Jumps up*) What you talking all about. Bodies? Bodies? You gonna be a hit man—for the Cosa Nostra? Man, what are you gonna do—eh? Fuck, is that what Goodwin is all about? Shit, I should've known better—hey! I'm not in this with you. (*Goes away, turns around*) How much is a hit?
Jay: Who said it was a hit?
Bernie: So! What is it man? (*Walks away*) Ah! I see you gonna ask for protection money or you gonna torch them buildings or wait a minute, you gonna kidnap someone's daughter and hold her for ransom—I know that's one of their favourite—shit, I get it—goddam—I can't believe it, Jay. Goodwin, eh, is that they guy who owns the laundromat on Park Ex, eh? You—hey, I'm not in this man. Next thing you know—I'd be fished out of the St. Laurent in a sack with a ton of cement chained to my feet . . .
Jay: Shut up!

Bernie: (*Silent, then after a while*) What's in it for me?

Jay: Did I say it was for free?

Bernie: Nope. 'cos, hey, you know I'm not working for free—listen man, (*Looks around furtively*) I still got my dad's piece with me.

Jay: Shut up—it's not a job.

Bernie: Ain't a job eh! O.K. So what the fuck is it?

Jay: (*Walks across the stage*) Listen, Goodwin knows (*Actress 2 gets up and gets curious*) some kids were carrying hygrade from Lebanon. Now somebody sang to the cops—so the family polished them off before the cops could get their hands on them, but the kids swallowed the shit—only Goodwin knows—and they were dropped off here at the edge of the moat last night—with holes in their heads.

Bernie: You mean, there are some stiffs lying around here! Shit man, whyn't you tell me before. (*Comes close to Jay*)

Jay: Bernie, you're like a tube light—you flicker before you come on.

Bernie: . . . (*Stares at Jay for a long time*) You gonna look for the corpses and pull the shit out, Jay! You can't do this man, that's rude shit—waking up the dead. You know the consequences man, they come back to haunt you—for the rest of your life. My uncle Rob once . . .

Jay: Shut up!

Bernie: Hey! So where are the corpses man . . .

Jay: Out there!

Shadow of a silhouetted woman

Bernie: Where? (*Whips around*)

Jay: There—somewhere—Goodwin's—he's gonna tell us the spot—we gotta dig 'em out.

Bernie: Dig 'em out eh—Hey, I done digging before. Oh Yeah! One time we had to dig this big safe out man—my aunt's place in Florida—it was a foot below the ground—you know—she'd hid it there 'cos my old uncle was stealing money from her all the time—so when she died . . .

Jay: Shut up. I hear something.
Bernie: What you hear man. (*Silent*) Yeah! Yeah! I hear something—sounds like somebody is coming this way . . . yeah!
Jay: Shut up and stay still.

They both huddle to one corner behind a ledge

Bernie: (*Points to cup and whispers*) You got anymore coffee there?
Jay: You finished it you jerk.
Bernie: Goddammitt, why do I keep finishing off the coffee, when I know there's none left.

Both look at each other

Bernie: Yeah! You're right—fuck, I'm useless man. I'm useless—I keep finishing off the coffee when I know there's none left and I know (*Starts bawling*) when it's gone, there's no money—to buy more man, 'cos fucking Molly . . .
Jay: Shut up . . .
Bernie: 'cos fucking Molly's been carrying out combin' operations through my pockets . . . shit.
Jay: Will you keep quiet.
Bernie: Of course I'll keep quiet man, I'll keep quiet when I get my skidoo and you gonna say "skidoo my ass" and I am gonna say yeah skidoo my ass, but I want it and I want it 'cos I wanna get out there far away—before the fucking snow melts, you know . . . (*Keeps raving and ranting . . .*)

At this point the window at the top opens and the silhouetted woman appears

Jay: (*Loud whisper*) Shut the fuck up with this skidoo shit, O.K. (*Gets a little out of control*)

Woman pours the water down—lights black out. Woman 2 on stage—up front—lights on her only—is seen shivering with cold. Her face is wet and the sound track is the sound of water pouring

from above.
Light spot on the 2. Jay and Bernie stand together at another corner, hand in pockets. Strange light on corpse.

Bernie: Jay! (*Clears his throat*) When I start counting everything I pass, I know I'm dying . . . and I know there are 14 Belcourt signs on the way here, 12 traffic lights and there are 128 windows in blue glass on the Mercantile Building and I know I'm dying man . . .

Jay: You're not dying man, you just trying to be intellectual and I don't care.

Bernie: Yeah, you're like that old woman up there in that highrise—take your shit and clear out.

Jay: Shut up Bernie, gee, how many times do I have to tell you to shut up in one night. (*Gap*) You had it all and you lost it all.

Bernie: My dad always said I was good for nothing—so I'd no chance—end up there . . .

Jay: Where?

Bernie: We was never rich, O.K.—I got nothing out of my parents—all my dad gave me was a lot of wopping in the ass—and all I got from my mom was bad teeth—so that what I say—I'll end up in hell—scratching in a living, making a crummy dollar.

Jay: Scaring away all the kids in Westmount park.

Bernie: (*Starts giggling*) Yeah, man—shit last Saturday night—I gelled my hair up man, and sat down on the bench—in the middle—right . . . like this (*Raises his eyes in a funny way*)

Jay: So?

Bernie: So these kids come in a slick european import right—and I'm sitting there—and I lift my eyes up like this right—they catch me on their high beam—fuck (*Starts laughing*) the kids never got out of the car man—you know they reversed and went straight out towards the mountain—man, I was looking like the white "Alpha Blondie" (*Goes into a laughing bout. . . . Stops*) At the end of this tho'—there is no fucking bread. (*Turns his pockets inside out*)

Jay: I don't think about it.

Bernie: Sure you don't think about it—you fucking think all the time but you like to say you don't think about it—huh! Everytime—it's you, you got new schemes coming out of your ears, you are the one who's thinking man—I quit thinking, I just follow—you the one who brought me here—man—now where'd you say are the stiffs? (*Scared*) Where's the has man—the big take huh?

Jay: Cool it Bernie (*Gets up*)

Bernie: Yeah, yeah, sure, cool it.

Jay: Bernie? (*Grin*)

Bernie: Yeah Jay.

Jay: We gotta look for the stiff.

Bernie: Yeah! You do it. I'll get more coffee (*Jay stops Bernie*)

Jay: You got no change—Goodwin's gonna be here any moment.

Bernie: I'll get some coffee.

Jay: No you won't.

Bernie: Give me some change.

Jay: Stay put right here.

At this point the window at the top opens and the silhouetted woman screams out in French: "Don't you have anything to do, you fucking dogs—take your shit and clear out of this neighbourhood."

SCENE 3

Two cops (MUC). One is sitting on edge of riser, reading a newspaper. The other one's got a nightstick—with which he is slapping his palm and walking around. Silence for a while.

Cop 2: I know for sure—this is the drop off point—

Cop 1: Settle down, if they're coming here, you'll hear them from a mile off.

Cop 2: We gotta have a game plan, man . . . otherwise they'll sneak out through the bushes.

Cop 1: Yeah! Yeah!

Cop 2: What do you mean yeah! yeah! Look, I don't want none of this laid back cool and easy shit. I wanna be ready and hot . . . (*He whips out his gun . . . checks it out and then puts it back*) Almost 60% of the murders in Quebec don't get solved 'cos there's no game plan, you know what I mean . . . you need a game plan—O.K.

Cop 1: (*Smiles at the audience and then at Cop 2*) What was your game plan last year when you had the big stake out in St. Leonard? Eh! For 5 hours you stuck it out in the bushes, sweating away—while the gang hit another Bank of Montreal branch—Hah!

Cop 2: Ok! Ok! That's enough, cut it out. What were you doing during the Stanley cup riot—twiddling your thumbs outside l'Annexe eh? Smilin' away at the rioters while the shoe store got looted. . . . Need a game plan . . . you know, a game plan . . .

Silence for a while

Cop 1: (*Starts whistling to himself and reading the paper*) Tabernac! You see this?

Cop 2: No, what?

Cop 1: Here look . . . they let him off . . .

Cop 2: Jesus!

Cop 1: Makes you mad, eh?

Cop 2: Damm right, it makes me mad. I knew it, I knew this was gonna happen.

Cop 1: Makes you wonder, what's the point eh? in being a cop. You nail the bastards, catch 'em red handed—but le maudit judge lets 'em off.

Cop 2: Shit, I knew it . . .

Cop 1: Manslaughter! Should have been first degree . . .

Cop 2: You're right . . . everytime you charge 'em first degree and then you plea bargain for a reduced charge . . .

Cop 1: . . . They get off the hook. . . . That's why I say you gotta have an air tight case.

Cop 2: . . . A game plan you know . . . got to plan the strategy, so it's an open and shut case . . . no witnesses . . .

Cop 1: This friend of this dude testified that he was so shocked when the gun went off . . . that his hands flew back . . .

Cop 2: Sure . . . hands flew back. . . . Now if that was one cop testifying for another . . . it wouldn't hold up in court. Everybody'd be shrieking murder.

Cop 1: Can you imagine if the kid was coloured and these two were cops.

Cop 2: And the cop would have to prove that his gun got cocked accidentally in the holster.

Cop 1: (*To audience*) That's what you call the double burden of being a cop . . . first of all everytime a cop uses a gun, he's suspect—and if the real suspect is coloured you're up shit creek . . . .

Cop 2: . . . in a leaky boat . . . without a paddle . . . (*Tugs his belt up*)

Gap

Cop 1: Just the other day, corner of St. Denis and Carré St. Louis . . .

Cop 2: Yeah!

Cop 1: Now I know the kid's gonna do the depanneur. So I'm watching him. Our eyes meet. The kid splits into the metro. I can't take my piece out, 'cos I'm not in a life threatening situation—so I chase him on foot and the fucker's lost.

Cop 2: Of course you gonna lose him. If I was you I'd put a bullet thru his brains in no time . . . fuck the witnesses man . . . the violence doesn't bother me, it's the mental pressure that's driving me up the wall.

Cop 1: You? Mental pressure?

Cop 2: I mean the kind of shit that's heaped up on us man . . . we got to learn their customs, their culture, their systems—shit, the voodoo mumbo jumbo . . . now what the fuck are they doing about us?

Cop 1: Nothing!

Cop 2: Yeah! Are they trying to understand our culture? Look man, here we don't send the cops to break the door down to beat your kid up, 'cos he hasn't brought the water back from the well—alright, they expect us to do it . . .

Cop 1: Visible Minority!

Cop 2: "Visible minority" my ass . . . what about us eh, . . . I get Somalia thinking about it.

Cop 1: You what?

Cop 2: Somalia . . . can't sleep at night.

Cop 1: Insomnia . . .

Cop 2: Yeah, Yeah, same thing . . . you know . . .

Cop 1: Yeah, we got to be careful . . . what we say, what we do.

Cop 2: Yeah, there's too many folks watching us and I'm tellin' you this Dunkin Donuts shit is getting on my nerves, brother.

Cop 1: What about Dunkin Donuts?

Cop 2: You know this shit about us spending too much time on Donuts. Every DJ on the air has a crack about where to find an MUC cop. . . . Yeah . . . where do they expect us to go for a break—in a strip bar or an ethnic Tunisian felafel joint? Eh? Hey, the Italian noodle place is as ethnic as I am willing to go . . . man . . . shit I'm hungry . . . let's go.

Lights fade and separate glow in corpse

Cop 1: (*Begins to leave, then stops*) Hang on.

Cop 2: What?

Cop 1: Stay cool, I thought I heard something move out there (*Whisper—both whip out their guns and cock them—lights glow on corpse*)

Cop 2: You cover me man (*Licks his tongue out . . . and moves sideways toward the back. . . . 1 watches him. He leaps over a riser and starts shouting*) Freeze—you crazy fucker, you had me fooled. . . . Don't move you ass hole. . . . One false move and you're dead, sucker. Hey, I said don't move . . .

Cop 1: Jeff . . . the man looks like he is dead already.

Cop 2: He is moving man. . . . I don't trust these fuckers . . . they are slippery . . . run a check on him Yves. . . . Don't move you fool.

Cop 1: Jeff. . . . He's not moving man . . . looks like he is all wrapped up.

Cop 2: I don't care. . . . I don't give a shit. . . . I'm not letting this one get away (*Gets very nervous*) I am gonna fix the fucker . . . lying low and watching us—you bastard (*Gets worked up and then finally ends up shooting the corpse*)

Cop 1: Jeff, what'd you do man . . .

Cop 2: Oh no, I shot the fucker, in the head. . .

Cop 1: Shit.

Cop 2: Oh No! Don't die on me . . . you fool, don't die on me . . . don't die on me (*Goes on bawling*)

Cop 1: (*Goes all around the stage . . . looking at the audience . . . in a panic . . .*) Jeff, you shot a corpse.

Woman 1 opens the window at the top. Lights out. Woman 1 had a red drop on her forehead—lights on her only. Woman at the window screams in Spanish "get the hell out of this neighbourhood" . . . blackout—music by band, base drum and cymbols.

SCENE 4

(Actor 1) Kalpesh comes in, in slightly ashen make-up. Half out of his original clothes. More agitated—a bit nervous—a bit furtive.

Kalpesh: Now, I hadn't finished and Ms. Nolan sneaked in. She's a good one, that. She sneaks into my territory 'cos she thinks I can embarrass the company—well hell, listen to this . . . the point I was making is that we are all actors, you are an actor, I am an actor—right this moment, you are acting as spectators. Yes, think about it—the point is we all have to become actors, not actors and spectators. That's what the barrier is all about—right, and we have to become actors in a larger context—we have to become protagonists in the world we live in . . . (*Actress 2 slowly rises. She has a staff in her hand. She moves towards him in a sideways movement*) . . . and not perpetuate the fucking myth about this unassailable tragic hero on stage who sports out all these unquestionable standards of life and liberty in the form of a saga . . .

Actress 2: "Isn't it tragic, we should come up here
And wanting nothing, but to get the bird,
Then be unable to find out the way?
For we, good audience, are sick with a disease
Quite the opposite to that which Sacas had,
A displaced person, whom no state would take
Until at last he elbowed into ours.

Kalpesh: You see what I mean! First we got to deal with this and then there is the added pain of staging it against all odds . . . so who's under wraps eh? Who's on the defensive?—us here . . . us, we are under wraps.

Actress 2: "The wise have but one god, wealth, little man.
All others are air, and empty talk.
For the shrines by my sire on the sea-shore founded
Destroy them, I care not—why tell me of these?

Kalpesh: (*Silent—face white*) Now, we are all trying to do theatre in a fresh, unconventional way? Agreed. We also do not want to arrive at obscure conclusions. Agreed. We do want to do popular theatre. Agreed. We do not however want to do theatre that is produced by the department for mirthlessness and artless propaganda. Good. We are propelled by our convictions to do agit prop. Good. Or are we? Are we headed for beggar's theatre, because we are beggars? Or would we continue to indulge in the breakdown of the formal stage, because we cannot afford it? Good question!

Actress 2: "This had happened before. I have been the victim of my reputation . . .
No sensible person should ever have his sons
Brought up more clever than the common run
Apart from being told they waste their time,
They earn the spite and envy of their neighbours."

Looks at him out of the corner of her eyes

Kalpesh: Oh, never mind. You see we do not have any money. Now that is the bottom line. We applied for a grant in Quebec city and they told us, "But excuse me, do you pay your artists?—we will consider a grant if you pay them." Well, jesus, how do you expect us to pay—isn't that what the grant is for? Now as we lick our wounds, while they pour more salt on them—we are constantly entrapped in a state of dealectical torpor. Formal stage or informal stage, Political theatre—mindless entertainment. Poor man's theatre—big bucks West Island musical, Living theatre or dead theatre (*Points to Actress 2*)

Actress 2: "My bones chill . . . "

Kalpesh: Now don't muck around with me. Listen. My time is short—Ms. Nolan could be here any moment. Why don't you go for vaudeville—instead of this—I mean even . . . listen, are you trying to impress me? I am not impressed. Listen. For years the audience was left theatreless—then enormous courage was rallied together to choose the path of popular theatre. So Brecht came along and knocked down the classics with a healthy disrespect. Now the bourgeois theatre is embalming Brecht as a classic. What a twist of history! Polly and MacHeath—remember (*Hums "mac the knife"*)—are now performed as big budget blockbusters, with music by David Bowie. Hah! And we are under wraps—under wraps—hustling for a deal where deals don't exist (*Shout. Slowly goes over to Actress 2 and puts his head on her shoulder*) . . . (*Sharp focus. Ms. Nolan appears after a while*)

Ms. Nolan: (*With headphones on*) Kalpesh!

Kalpesh: Yes, Ms. Nolan—that's it for me (*To audience*) I'm leaving—I thought there (*Starts leaving*) was a lull in the action and besides I thought you were in the sound booth.

Ms. Nolan: (*To the audience*) It's pointless apologising for him now, because despite our best efforts -

Kalpesh: There's no need to apologise Ms. Nolan. . . . I've already informed the whole audience. . . . I haven't told them tho' about "that talkative Indian" bit—will you please say it . . . . or can I say it for you? (*clears his throat*)

Actress 2: "I am not afraid to say, that these who seem
Wise among men and accomplished talkers
Must pay the heaviest penalty of all.
No mortal man is happy. He might grow
More prosperous, if fortune came his way,
Than others, but happy he can never be."

Ms. Nolan: Kalpesh, before I . . .

Kalpesh: Fling those headphones. . . . Ms. Nolan—I am leaving this stage . . . but tell me how come you let her roll off those corny lines from Euripides, jesus christ . . . (*Starts to back out through the alley slowly*)

Ms. Nolan: She is presentable—you are not.

Kalpesh: Not presentable, I don't believe this—I don't believe this and the audience has nothing to say.

Ms. Nolan: You have no business to disrupt this show.

Kalpesh: I should be put under wraps? Eh? (*To audience*) Because I am not a professional, right? Because I've exhausted the role of the joker.

Ms. Nolan: Kalpesh!

Actress 2 becomes agitated and slightly alarmed—paces back and forth on her riser.

Kalpesh: My presence has never been in doubt. I am everywhere all the time, but now my status is suspect.

Ms. Nolan: Kalpesh, this is outrageous.

Kalpesh: This is not outrageous. You are just trying to overpower me.

Ms. Nolan: You should be, you should be put away.

Kalpesh: (*Backing through the alley*) This is it. If I don't sing and dance to an ethnic beat I must be put away. I am not professional, right—because I am not a main liner, right—because I am a fringe fucker, right . . . because I am ethnic and therefore I should be multicultural only, right . . . (*Trails out*)

SCENE 5

Two women journalists—one of them is pretending to throw stone chips on the water—sound effect

J.1: Moose walked into my neighbour's pool this afternoon.
J.2: What?
J.1: A moose walked into my neighbour's pool.
J.2: You're kidding. (*Silence*) And . . . so what happened?
J.1: Nothin'
J.2: Nothing?
J.1: It's still there.
J.2: What?
J.1: Yup . . . still there.
J.2: And? . . . is it stuck?
J.1: Nope, just can't get out. Need a helicopter to truss it up. Nobody wants to pay for it.
J.2: What about the SPCA?
J.1: They are generally not in favour of animals getting trussed up in the air.
J.2: Oh! So what's gonna happen? . . . I mean . . . is there water in the pool?
J.1: Of course . . . what do you think . . . anyway, it's an unimportant issue . . . the reason why I brought you here . . .
J.2: Now wait a minute. . . Jennifer . . .
J.1: The reason why I got you here . . . .
J.2: Just a minute—you're trivializing the whole issue and me . . . I am concerned . . .
J.1: About moose?
J.2: Jennifer . . . you've just told me that a moose has fallen into the neighbour's pool . . .
J.1: Right.
J.2: Now. . . I am concerned . . .
J.1: Why?
J.2: I am concerned because . . . for one thing, where did this moose come from . . . there aren't too many moose in this

area . . .

J.1: And second of all?

J.2: I have a pool.

J.1: YOU HAVE A POOL!

J.2: Yes, I have a pool and I would like to know what to do in the event of a moose-in-the-pool situation.

J.1: None. . . . You just hope the FM96 traffic helicopter spots it from the sky and alerts the fire department who will come . . . and

J.2: Jennifer!

J.1: . . . or one of our South Shore reporters

J.2: Now wait a minute . . . .

J.1: I am not trivializing the issue . . . I am just trying to tell you that this just might turn out to be the headlines for tomorrow.

J.2: Sure the headlines for tomorrow! and not the story on the Philippines . . . the new coup in the works . . . incidentally . . .

J.1: It will get killed . . . compared to the moose in Brossard. It doesn't stand a chance. . . .

J.2: What about the "extra" on the IMF story in Mexico.

J.1: (*Slowly turns around*) Oh come on Judith. . . . Right in the middle of the drought in Mozambique that was killing 200 people a day—our headline was "Alliance Quebec leader swallows bitter pill—Daughter must go to French School."

J.2: You're right—we seem to pick up on this shit all the time and blow it up out of proportion. (*She also starts throwing the rocks into the water*) So what with this big moonlight rendezvous . . . is there something you wanted to tell me?

J.1: Yeah, yeah . . . the reason why I got you here is 'cos . . .

J.2: Why?

J.1: (*Sits down on the railing*) There's a story that's scheduled to break this evening here . . . if we file our reports by 1—it just might make the lead on the front page.

J.2: (*Gets up*) Here? You gotta be kidding.

J.1: There's a speedboat headed here anytime . . . now . . . (*whisper*)

J.2: Yeah?

J.1: And it's loaded with five corpses.

J.2: What? 5 corpses? What are you talking about?

J.1: Yeah, 5 stiffs stashed with hash!

J.2: Stashed with hash! Eh?

J.1: I got the inside dope on it . . . (*Smiles and walks about*) . . . there's some guys who know the stiffs are worth—5 million—1 million per stiff street value.

J.2: So they gonna stake out the boat and snatch the stiffs!

J.1: Shit! You got it right . . . and I wanna stake 'em out and get the story.

J.2: You got a flash for your camera? . . . (*Chewing gum ferociously*)

J.1: (*Fishes out small device*) Infra-red view finder, sistuh . . . it photographs by starlight.

J.2: Geez, Jen . . . you're hi tech tonight. (*Gap*) So, how come you had me going on the moose story?

J.1: Just keeping you awake.

J.2: Oh! I see.

Silence for a while. 1 stares

J.2: So . . . what's next—what you thinking about now . . . hey, Jen? I hate this shit . . . when you start looking out like that. What now?

J.1: I was just thinking—if it ain't death, it's diseases, if it ain't disease it's destruction—the media's got the big d's going on every page . . .

J.2: (*Gap*) . . . and if it ain't destruction it's drugs. You're right . . . one more "d"—just being participatory. Wanna gum?

At this point the window opens lights off, woman speaks in Italian this time.

SCENE 6

Lead TV Evangelist comes walking through the alley. Black cape on. . . . Followed by 2nd Evangelist. First one comes and puts one leg up on one riser. Looks a bit nervous and disturbed. Second one comes up to him timidly.

E.2: Tonight's the night!

E.1: (*Wipes sweat with handkerchief*) Hallelujah! Tonight's the night. The lord Jesus had never been unkind to me. He knows me—he knows I heal at his will, I care for his children, I love them because he wants me to, I touch them because his desire is mine, hallelujah.

E.2: Hallelujah! Praise the lord.

E.1: "I tell you this, that for every unfounded word men utter, they will answer on Judgement day, since it is by your words you will be acquitted, and by your words condemned."

E.2: Matthew, Book 12 Verse 22.

Silence for a while as 1 paces once across the stage and comes back to the riser.

E.2: Tonight's the night reverend.

E.1: The dead shall rise. You will see brother Pierre, there is but one God and he has spoken to me in a level and conversational voice. (*Eyes closed*) Hallelujah! He has appeared to me atop a mountain of clouds and has said to me, "Pat, you sinned once at the Town Squire Motor Inn & Lodge on St. Jacques. This is your choice Pat. Go to the moat by the Rive Sud and there you shall find atonement for your sins. Souls have to be raised. Bodies have to be cleansed." In a short time, my star will rise again, Pierre. The lord Jesus said, "in a short time you will no longer see me, and then a short time later you will see me again."

E.2: John Book 16, Verse 8. Praise the lord and the Rive Sud.

E.1: For go into where the dead lie and raise them from their drugs, sex and rock and roll inspired death.

E.2: Luke Book 7, Verse 9.

E.1: Is it . . . ?

E.2: Let me check. (*Pulls out small bible . . . can't find it*) Maybe it's reversed reverend. Sex and drugs and rock 'n roll instead of drugs, sex and rock and roll?

E.1: Raise them lord, from this deathly disease, save their souls, lord and bring me back my peace, hallelujah.

E.2: Hallelujah! But reverend, what if they are too far dead . . . do you have any other plans?

E.1: Pierre, I brought in my boats, landed the soldiers and burned the boats behind them. There is no turning back for me Pierre. It's either this, or I lose my slot on 4 Saison. Sunday Morning.

E.2: What a joy it is to be here with you. Such tremendous zeal and determination! Hallelujah! Thank the lord, God bless you all (*To audience*) Rev Pat will raise the dead, here on Rive Sud . . . the devil and his disciples who have infested this land with foreign drug smugglers and temptresses operating out of motels will be cursed and driven to distraction . . .

E.1: Now people have asked me—Pat, what will happen if you cannot atone for you sins. I have told the lord in an unemotional and calm voice—"Lord, I need your support—I have sinned—I have sinned against you lord, against my wife, my children, and my entire TV congregation (*Cries*) I have no plan B lord. I only have plan A. I have no plan B lord, because plan B is for wimps, my lord. (*Gets angry*) Plan B is for those who want a 2nd rate congregation, with a 2nd rate economy, burdened with debt, unbridled spending, a congregation with broken families, plagued with drugs and a congregation that supports the induction of queers into the profession. . . . I have only plan A, lord.

E.2: Hallelujah, praise the lord and the plan!

E.1: (*Striding across the stage*) I have a plan A, Pierre—a plan A only will wipe out this evil empire in our midst—and the lord willing we shall see the end of this perestroika crap that has got everybody all excited. Reform, my ass. We don't need it—we are fine without it. They need it. They shall get it. I have seen their tricks before and believe me, hallelujah, this time I shall roll the tanks—the tanks of the lord into their evil midst and cleanse them with the sweet salvas from sweet Jesus, our lord. "He who is not with me is against me, and he who does not gather with me scatters."

E.2: Luke Book 2, Verse 36, Hallelujah.

E.1: I have a plan A that will uplift this congregation—this drug infested swamp and bring it back to life. I will raise funds, build new houses for the lord and bring peace in our midst. Amen.

E.2: Hallelujah! Praise the lord.

Rev. Pat takes out tooth brush and tooth paste and starts brushing his teeth.

E.1: I love the lord and I love a man who's not ready to compromise. We're living in a land of wimps, I say Rev. Pat's gonna make a difference, you'll see. He's a christian soldier and he aint taking no prisoners. For too long, the sins of man have been blamed on the lord. In the book of revelations it is said, "Come here and I will show the punishment given to the famous prostitute who rules enthroned beside abundant waters—the one with whom all the kings of the earth have committed fornification and who has made all the population of the world drunk with the wine of her adultery."

E.2: (*Stops brushing his teeth—clears his throat*) The woman was dressed in purple and scarlet and glittered with gold and jewels and pearls and she was holding a wine cup filled with the disgusting filth of her fornification, on her forehead was written a name, a cryptic name "Babylon the great, the mother of all the prostitutes and all the filthy practices on the earth. . . .

At this point, the lights dim and the woman in the window appears . . . she slowly tears them apart as before in Punjabi this time. Blackout.

SCENE 7

As music fades from previous scene—glow on corpse is seen. Bernie comes in through the alley holding a flashlight. Blue light comes in through alley. Jay is seen sitting on the riser. Soft glow.

Jay: It's gotta be here, somewhere, man. (*Loud whisper*) I ain't givin' up.
Bernie: Fuck, hope no one pulls a trick on us man.
Jay: No one knows 'cept Goodwin and us, ok!

Bernie makes a wide detour up front of audience—so that the alley light shows them up as silhouette.

Bernie: Hey! (*Spots the corpse*) Jaaaaaaaay! You see what I see man. . . . Is that it?
Jay: What? Yeah . . . that's it . . . how'd it get there?
Bernie: You're fucking crazy, bringing me here . . . man. . . . I wanna go, Jay can I . . . .
Jay: No you can't! (*Closing in on corpse*)
Bernie: Why are we whispering?
Jay: I don't know why we are whispering . . . just shut up. (*In low posture*)
Bernie: Why are we crouching?
Jay: Because you're scared . . . you asshole.
Bernie: My dad said anytime you're scared . . .
Jay: Now will you shut up.

Jay reaches corpse—Bernie stays away. Jay pulls the corpse out from behind the garbage can and brings it center front. Lights glow to a larger area around center front. Bernie comes closer slowly. They are both slowly removing the layers around the corpse. Music. Jay pulls out a knife. Back to the audience.

Jay: This is it man!
Bernie: Hey! That's easy man—I can do that . . . (*After a while*) Shit—man (*Starts doing it on his own excitedly*)

Jay goes off to take a leak in the alley.

Jay: You got the hang of it.
Bernie: Hey, Jay the fucking stiff's warm man . . .

Jay: Keep going man—keep going . . .
Bernie: I'm telling you it feels warm . . .
Jay: Bernie, you're the self-appointed pope of bad taste—that stiff's been cold for 2 days, ok?
Bernie: Hey Jay, it's movin' man . . .
Jay: It's not movin', pea brain . . . it's called rigor mortis . . .

At this point, the corpse's knee folds. Bernie drops the knife and is about to leap away . . . the hand from the corpse grabs his ankles.

Bernie: Jay! . . . (*Screams and cries out to Jay. Corpse sits up and mutters a laugh*)
Jay: Oh fuck . . . it's . . . it's . . . I . . . .
Bernie: Let me go . . . (*Scream*)

Music. Corpse's face is barely visible.

Jay: Oh fuck!
Corpse: Oh fuck is right, come here! Unwrap me you silly discontented native . . . (*Laugh*) Give me a few more seconds of your empire. . . . Hah! And I shall have a monument built for me. A cultural monument. (*Unfolds himself slowly. Jay comes closer. Bernie slides out crawling*) I tell you what! Unwrap me and you shall see . . . a cynical, subversive, disoriented oriental, who refuses to fight the correct battles in the correct language. Unwrap me and you will find a bastard youth sporting a dubbed version of the classics. Unwrap me and you shall see a colored Johnny Rotten telling the CBC live to fuck off 'cos they want script writers from the visible minorities. They got grants for that you know! Unwrap me and you shall find a photo-blow-up of a rock and roll rightover from the mysterious east, whose beat extends beyond the ethnic alley. Unwrap me and you shall find a pace-setter from Gujarat, India whose only fault is he likes theatre but can make a living elsewhere as well.

Lights off. Now a music theme develops in the background. Again lights come on—Kalpesh is covered in center stage. Under quick change of color gels—corpse lies covered.

Evangelist: The name of the game is "Name that miracle" or "Boob tube Healin' made to order." (*Laughs*) Mind you, Charisma can be had on the CRT if the viewer is up for it—and the average viewer is always up for it—Heal! Satani—get out of this body. Hallelujah, praise the lord—'cos miracles are just a . . .

Woman journalist: Sleight of hand. . . . A subject in the head can bend objects in the hand . . . depends . . . now which one came first—the subject or the object . . . the ruler? Or the divisive incident? The editorial or the . . . (*Freezes in horror*)

Cop 1: Oh mon dieu . . . what a mess. Now who could have done that. . . . Jesus! Tsk, tsk. (*Gap*) Now, intellectuals are cute—train the pigs they say, teach 'em sociology 101, Urban Affairs 202, Jah-Make-Yah 303. . . . But when it comes to the crunch, when you're walking the beat . . . the odds are stacked . . .

Actress 1: (*In the window, hands folded—side view*) Nope, it ain't, now dig this man, the dude was right—you can hustle or you can create, but you can't do both. . . . Ok? . . . so if you hustle you can't create and if you can't create you die. That's the bottom line—you're under wraps. The dude was right.

Woman 1: Yes, there's money for folklore, there's money for the pros. If you're ethnic on top of that, there's no escaping the multicultural crap. But an ethnic pro? Est!! Get the hell out of this neighbourhood. Ok.

Jay: In the fist of the night,
When the silence is right,
A power hold grips the neighbourhood,
. . . .

Band breaks into the song. Blackout.

Bows